Jekka's
COTTAGE GARDEN HERBS

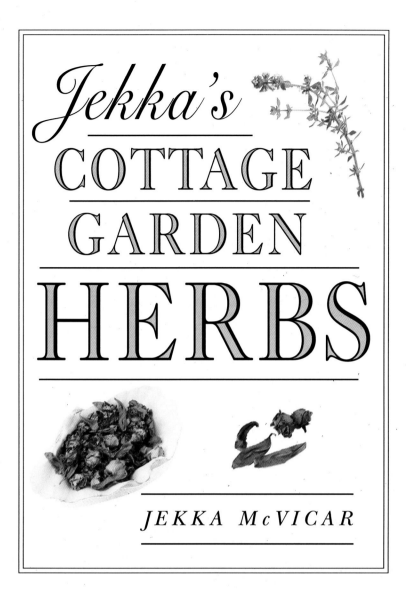

Jekka's COTTAGE GARDEN HERBS

JEKKA McVICAR

KYLE CATHIE LIMITED

To Alistair

First published as *Jekka's Cottage Garden Herbs*
in Great Britain in 1995 by
Kyle Cathie Limited
20 Vauxhall Bridge Road, London SW1V 2SA

This edition published 1995

ISBN 1 85626 208 1

2 4 6 8 10 9 7 5 3 1

The material in this book is taken from
Jekka's Complete Herb Book

Book design by Geoff Hayes
Cover design by Tom Murdoch and Geoff Hayes

Printed and bound in Spain
by Graficas Reunidas, S.A., Madrid.

Jessica McVicar is hereby identified as the author of this
work in accordance with Section 77 of the Copyright,
Designs and Patents Act, 1988.

A Cataloguing in Publication record for this title is available
from the British Library.

Acknowledgements
With many thanks to Mac for all his support, Anthea for
turning up in the nick of time, Kyle for taking the gamble,
Piers for all his reading and Penny for her compliments.

Photographic acknowledgements
Plant photography by Jekka McVicar and Sally Maltby.
All other photography by Michelle Garrett.

CONTENTS

INTRODUCTION

'Here's flowers for you;
Hot lavender, mints, savory, marjoram,
The marigold, that goes to bed wi' the sun,
And with him rises weeping.'
Shakespeare

Herbs have been used since man has been on Earth as a food and a medicine. There are few plants capable of providing the sheer pleasure of herbs, they are the most generous of plants, aromatic and attractive, useful in both the home and the garden, health-giving and healthy.

The increasing interest in herbs is part of a movement towards a healthier lifestyle, symbolising a more natural approach. Herbs are used in cooking, in domestic products, alternative medicines and cosmetics, and they affect the quality of life in many ways.

The most extraordinary feature of herbs is their incredible versatility. You may think of a particular herb as having mainly culinary or medicinal properties and then discover it has other useful applications. Thyme, for example, provides the raw material for cooking, medicines and aromatherapy.

What is a herb? It can be argued that all useful plants are herbs. The Oxford English Dictionary defines them as 'Plants of which the leaves, stem or flowers are used for food or medicine, or in some way for their scent or flavour'. To elaborate, a herb can be any plant used as an ingredient in food or drink for flavour or preservative properties, in medicine for health-giving properties, or in perfume, cosmetics or aromatherapy as a fixative, for flavour or aroma or as a cleansing agent. That herbs do you good is in no doubt, improving your health, appearance or sense of well-being.

With gardens becoming nostalgic, and the re-surge in interest in the cottage garden one will find that herbs are most useful plants to incorporate into the overall design, not only do they look pretty, for who can resist the gold face of the Pot Marigold, or the heady aroma of the Sweet Rocket in the evening, or watch a cat nibbling at the catnip and then lying in shear heavenly bliss, but they are edible as well. Oregano with its profusion of pale mauve/pink flowers is covered in butterflies in summer, whereas in spring and autumn it is an indispensable culinary herb. Wild strawberry with its delicate white flowers in spring to early summer produces delectable small sweet strawberries which are lovely to eat on their own or added to pies or to flavour syrups. So whether you use them or not, by planting them you will add another dimension to the garden and re-create a little haven of the past. A tip worth noting is, that if you do wish to pick them regularly to use either in the kitchen or medicinally, some stepping stones placed in the garden, will make accessability easy and also keep your feet clean during the wet times of the year. A plus to regularly picking is that herbs will not take over the garden and will keep flowering for longer. Do not forget that the flowers of Anise Hyssop, Pot Marigolds, Sweet Rocket, Honey Suckle, Pinks, to name but a few, are edible as well as attractive.

When planning a herb garden there are no restrictions on how it should be laid out , formally or informally, as a border, or in a pot. The only factors you must consider are; what are the soil conditions like? How sunny or shady is the area you have chosen? Would this suit the herbs you want to plant? If you find the area unsuitable for a particular herb and you have no wish to re-design your garden, plant them in containers as you will find that most herbs are accommodating plants and will grow happily in them as long as you take due consideration of their root size.This then frees you to place them in the position that most suits them and yours design. If necessary sinking the pots into the soil to disguise them. Bearing in mind that this is a cottage garden you may wish to incorporate some herbs into an already established border, it is therefore important to make sure that you take note of the height and width of each herb, so you can place it in the best position to enhance your garden and gain the most beneficially aspects of the herb. Finally I must stress that all herbs grown for either culinary or medicinal use should be grown free from the use of chemicals.

Jekka McVicar

PROPAGATION

One of the great joys of gardening is propagating your own plants. Success is dependent on adequate preparation and the care and attention you give during the critical first few weeks. The principles remain the same, but techniques are constantly changing. There is always something new to discover.

The three main methods of propagating new plants are by Seed, Cuttings and Layering.

This chapter provides general, step-by-step instructions for each of these methods. As there are always exceptions to a rule, please refer to the propagation section under each individual herb.

SEED

Sowing Outside
Most annual herbs grow happily propagated year after year from seed sown directly into the garden. There are two herbs worth mentioning where that is not the case – sweet marjoram, because the seed is so small it is better started in a pot; and basil because, in damp northern climates like that in Britain, the young seedlings will rot off.

In an average season the seed should be sown in mid- to late spring after the soil has been prepared and warmed. Use the arrival of weed seedlings in the garden as a sign that the temperature is rising. Herbs will survive in a range of different soils. Most culinary herbs originate from the Mediterranean so their preference is for a sandy free-draining soil. If your soil is sticky clay do not give up, give the seeds a better start by adding a fine layer of horticultural sand along the drill when preparing the seed bed.

Preparation of Seed Bed
Before starting, check your soil type making sure that the soil has sufficient food to maintain a seed bed. Dig the bed over, mark out a straight line with a piece of string secured tightly over each row, draw a shallow drill, 6-13mm (¼/½in) deep, using the side of a fork or hoe, and sow the seeds thinly, 2 or 3 per 25mm (1in). Do not overcrowd the bed, otherwise the seedlings will grow leggy and weak and be prone to disease.

Protected Sowing
Starting off the seeds in a greenhouse or on a windowsill gives you more control over the warmth and moisture they need, and enables you to begin propagating earlier in the season.

Nothing is more uplifting than going into the greenhouse on a cold and gloomy late-winter morning and seeing all the seedlings emerging. It makes one enthusiastic for spring.

Preparation of Seed
Most seeds need air, light, temperature and moisture to germinate. Some have a long dormancy, and some have hard outer coats and need a little help to get going. Here are two techniques.

Scarification
If left to nature, seeds that have a hard outer coat would take a long time to germinate. To speed up the process, rub the seed between 2 sheets of fine sandpaper. This weakens the coat of the seed so that moisture essential for germination can penetrate.

Stratification (vernalization)
Some seeds need a period of cold (from 1 to 6 months) to germinate. Mix the seed with damp sand and place in a plastic bag in the refrigerator or freezer. After 4 weeks sow on the surface of the compost and cover with Perlite. My family always enjoys this time of year. They go to the freezer to get the ice cream and find herb seed instead.

Preparation of Seed Container
One of the chief causes of diseased compost is a dirty propagation container. To minimize the spread of disease, remove any 'tidemarks' of compost, soil or chemicals around the insides of the pots and seed trays. Wash and scrub them thoroughly with washing up liquid, rinse with water and give a final rinse with diluted Jeyes fluid. Leave for 24 hours before re-use. Old compost also provides ideal conditions for damping off fungi and sciarid flies. To avoid cross-infection always remove spent compost from the greenhouse or potting shed.

Compost
It is always best to use a sterile seed compost. Ordinary garden soil contains many weed seeds that could easily be confused with the germinating herb seed. The compost used for most seed sowing is 50per cent propagating bark and 50per cent peat-based seed compost and unless stated otherwise within the specific herb section, this is the mix to use. However, for herbs that

Misting Unit

prefer a freer draining compost, or for those that require stratification outside, I advise using a 25 per cent peat-based seed compost: 50 per cent propagating bark and 25 per cent horticultural grit mix. And if you are sowing seeds that have a long germination period, use a soil-based seed compost.

Sowing in Seed Trays
Preparation: fill a clean seed tray with compost up to 1cm (½in) below the rim and firm down with a flat piece of wood. Do not to press too hard as this will over-compress the compost and restrict drainage, encouraging damping off disease and attack by sciarid fly.

The gap below the rim is essential, as it prevents the surface sown seeds and compost being washed over the edge when watering, and it allows room for growth when you are growing under card or glass.

Water the prepared tray using a fine rose on the watering can. Do not over-water. The compost should be damp, not soaking. After an initial watering, water as little as possible, but never let the surface dry out. Once the seed is sown lack of moisture can prevent germination and kill the seedlings, but too much water excludes oxygen and encourages damping-off fungi and root rot. Be sure to use a fine rose on the watering can so as not to disturb the seed.

Sowing Methods
There are 3 main methods, the choice dependent on the size of the seed. They are, in order of seed size, fine to large:

1 Scatter on the surface of the compost, and cover with a fine layer of Perlite.

2 Press into the surface of the compost, either with your hand or a flat piece of wood the size of the tray,

and cover with Perlite.
3 Press down to 1 seed's depth and cover with compost.

The Cardboard Trick
When seeds are too small to handle, you can control distribution by using a thin piece of card (cereal cartons are good), cut to 10cm x 5cm (4in x 2in), and folded down the middle. Place a small amount of seed into the folded card and gently tap it over the prepared seed tray. This technique is especially useful when sowing into plug trays (see below).

Sowing in Plug (Module) Trays (Multi-cell Trays)
These plug trays are a great invention. The seed can germinate in its own space, get established into a strong seedling, and make a good root ball. When potting on, the young plant remains undisturbed and will continue growing, rather than coming to a halt because it has to regenerate roots to replace those damaged in pricking out from the seed tray. This is very good for plants like coriander, which hate being transplanted and tend to bolt if you move them. Another advantage is that as you are sowing into individual cells, the problem of overcrowding is cut to a minimum, and damping-off disease and sciarid fly are easier to control. Also, because seedlings in plugs are easier to maintain, planting out or potting on is not so critical.

Plug trays come in different sizes; for example, you can get trays with very small holes of 15mm (½in) x

15mm up to trays with holes of 36.5mm (1¼in) x 36.5mm. To enable a reasonable time lapse between germination and potting on, I recommend the larger.

When preparing these trays for seed sowing, make sure you have enough space, otherwise compost seems to land up everywhere. Prepare the compost and fill the tray right to the top, scraping off surplus compost with a piece of wood level with the top of the holes. It is better not to firm the compost down. Watering in (see above) settles the compost enough to allow space for the seed and the top dressing of Perlite. For the gardener-in-a-hurry there are available in good garden centres ready-prepared propagation trays, which are plug trays already filled with compost. All you have to do is water and add the seed.

The principles of sowing in plug trays are the same as for trays. Having sown your seed, DO label the trays clearly with the name of the plant, and also the date. The date is useful as one can check their late or speedy germination. It is also good for record keeping, if you want to sow them again next year, and helps with organizing the potting on.

Seed Germination
Seeds need warmth and moisture to germinate.

The main seed sowing times are autumn and spring. This section provides general information with the table below providing a quick look guide to germination. Any detailed advice specific to a particular herb is provided in the A-Z Herb section.

Quick Germination Guide
Hot 27-32°C (80-90°F)
Rosemary

Warm 15-21°C (60-70°F)
Most plants, including those from the Mediterranean, and Chives and Parsley.

Cool 4-10°C (40-50°F)
Lavenders. (Old lavender seed will need a period of stratification).

Stratification
Arnica (old seed), Sweet Woodruff, Yellow Iris, Poppy, Soapwort, Sweet Cicely, Hops (old seed), Sweet Violet.

Scarification
All leguminous species, i.e., broom, trefoils, clovers and vetches.

Need Light (i.e., do not cover)
Chamomile, Foxglove, Thyme, Winter Savory, Poppy and Sweet Marjoram.

In a cold greenhouse, a heated propagator may be needed in early spring for herbs that germinate at warm to hot temperatures. In the house you can use a shelf near a radiator (never on the radiator), or an airing cupboard. Darkness does not hinder the germination of most herbs (see table above for exceptions), but if you put your containers in an airing cupboard YOU MUST CHECK THEM EVERY DAY. As soon as there is any sign of life, place the trays in a warm light place, but not in direct sunlight.

Hardening Off
When large enough to handle, prick out seed tray seedlings and pot up individually. Allow them to root fully.

Test plug tray seedlings by giving one or two a gentle tug. They should come away from the cells cleanly, with the root ball. If they do not, leave for another few days.

When the seedlings are ready, harden them off gradually by leaving the young plants outside during the day. Once weaned into a natural climate, either plant them directly into a prepared site in the garden, or into a larger container for the summer.

CUTTINGS

Taking cuttings is sometimes the only way to propagate (e.g. non-flowering herbs, such as **Chamomile Treneague**, and variegated forms, such as Tri-color Sage).

It is not as difficult as some people suggest, and even now I marvel at how a mere twig can produce roots and start the whole life cycle going again.

There are 4 types of cutting used in herb growing:

1 Softwood cuttings taken in spring

2 Semi-hardwood cuttings taken in summer

3 Hardwood cuttings taken in autumn

4 Root cuttings, which can be taken in spring and autumn.

For successful softwood cuttings it is worth investing in a heated propagator, which can be placed either in a greenhouse or on a shady windowsill. For success-ful semi-ripe, hardwood and root cuttings, a shaded cold frame can be used.

Softwood Cuttings
Softwood cuttings are taken from the new lush green growth of most perennial herbs between spring and mid-summer, a few examples being Balm of Gilead, Bergamot, the Chamomiles, the Mints, Prostanthera, the Rosemarys, the Scented Geraniums, the Thymes, Curly Wood Sage and Wormwood. Check under the individual herb entries in the A-Z section for more specific information.

1 The best way to get a plant to produce successful rooting material is to prune it vigorously in winter (which will encourage rapid growth when the temperature rises in the spring), and to take cuttings as soon as there is sufficient growth.

2 Fill a pot, seed tray, or plug tray with cutting compost – 50 per cent bark, 50 per cent peat. It is important to use a well-draining medium rather than standard potting mixes as, without root systems, cuttings are prone to wet rot.

Firm the compost to within 2cm (¾in) of the rim.

If space is limited or pots are unavailable, you can pack the base of several cuttings in damp sphagnum moss (rolled up firmly in a polythene strip and held in place by a rubber band or string) until the roots form.

3 Collect the cuttings in small batches in the morning. Choose sturdy shoots with plenty of leaves. Best results come from non-flowering shoots with the base leaves removed. Cut the shoot with a knife, not scissors. This is because scissors tend to pinch or seal the end of the cutting thus hindering rooting.

4 Place the cutting at once in the shade in a polythene bag or a bucket of water. Softwood cuttings are extremely susceptible to water loss; even a small loss will hinder root development. If the cuttings cannot be dealt with quickly, keep them in the cool (e.g. in a salad box from a refrigerator) to prevent excessive water loss.

5 To prepare the cutting material, cut the base of the stem 5mm (¼in) below a leaf joint, to leave a cutting of roughly 10cm (4in) long.

6 If the cutting material has to be under 10cm (4in), take the cutting with a heel. Remove the lower leaves and trim the tail which is left from the heel.

7 Trim the stem cleanly before a node, the point at which a leaf stalk joins the stem. Remove the leaves from the bottom third of the cutting, leaving at least 2 or 3 leaves on top. The reason for leaving leaves on cuttings is that the plant feeds through them as it sets root. Do not tear off the base leaves as this can cause disease; use a knife and gently cut them off.

8 Make a hole with a dibber in the compost and insert the cutting up to its leaves. Make sure that the leaves do not touch or go below the surface of the compost; they will rot away and may cause a fungus condition which can spread up the stem and to other cuttings. Do not overcrowd the container or include more than one species, because quite often they take different times to root. (For instance, keep box and thymes separate.)

Hormone rooting-powders that some gardeners use, contain synthetic plant hormones and fungicide and are not for the organic grower; following my detailed instructions you should find them unnecessary. However, they may help with difficult cuttings. The cutting should be dipped into the rooting-powder just before inserting into the compost.

9 Label and date the cuttings clearly, and only water the compost from above if necessary (the initial watering after preparing the container should be sufficient). Keep out of direct sunlight in hot weather. In fact, if it is very sunny, heavy shade is best for the first week.

Either place in a heated or unheated propagator, or cover the pot or container with a plastic bag supported on a thin wire hoop (to prevent the plastic touching the leaves), or with an upturned plastic bottle with the bottom cut off. If you are using a plastic bag, make sure you turn it inside out every few days to stop excess moisture from condensation dropping onto the cuttings.

10 Spray the cuttings every day with water for the first week. Do this in the morning, never at night. Do not test for rooting too early by tugging the cutting up, as you may disturb it at a crucial time. A better way to check for new roots is to look underneath the container. Average rooting time is 2-4 weeks.

The cutting medium is low in nutrients, so give a regular foliar feed when the cutting starts to root.

11 Harden off the cuttings gradually when they are rooted. Bring them out in stages to normal sunny, airy conditions.

12 Pot them on using a prepared potting compost once they are weaned. Label and water well after transplanting.

13 About 4-5 weeks after transplanting, when you can see that the plant is growing away, pinch out the top centre of the young cutting. This will encourage the plant to bush out, making it stronger as well as fuller.

14 Allow to grow on until a good-size root ball can be seen in the pot – check occasionally by gently removing the plant from the pot – then plant out.

Semi-hardwood Cuttings or Greenwood Cuttings
Usually taken from shrubby herbs such as Rosemary and Myrtle towards the end of the growing season (from mid-summer to mid-autumn). Use the same method (steps 2-8) as for softwood cuttings, with the following exceptions:

2 The compost should be freer-draining than for softwood cuttings, as semi-hardwood cuttings will be left for longer (see 10 below). Make the mix equal parts peat, grit and bark.

9 Follow step 9 for softwood cuttings, but place the pot, seed tray or plug tray in a cold greenhouse, cold frame, cool conservatory, or on a cold windowsill in a garage, not in a propagator, unless it has a misting unit.

10 Average rooting time for semi-hardwood cuttings is 4-6 weeks. Follow step 10 except for the watering schedule. Instead, if the autumn is exceptionally hot and the compost or cuttings seem to be drying out, spray once a week. Again, do this in the morning, and be careful not to over-water.

11 Begin the hardening off process in the spring after the frosts. Give a foliar feed as soon as there is sufficient new growth.

Hardwood Cuttings
Taken mid- to late autumn in exactly the same way as softwood cuttings steps 2-8, but with a freer draining compost of equal parts peat, grit and bark. Keep watering to the absolute minimum. Winter in a cold frame, greenhouse or conservatory. Average rooting time can take as long as 12 months.

Root Cuttings
This method of cutting is suitable for plants with creeping roots, such as Bergamot, Comfrey, Horseradish, Lemon Balm, Mint. Soapwort and Sweet Woodruff.

1 Dig up some healthy roots in spring or autumn.

2 Fill a pot, seed tray or plug tray with cutting compost – 50 per cent bark, 50 per cent peat, firmed to within 3cm (1in) of the rim. Water well and leave to stand while preparing your cutting material.

3 Cut 4-8cm (1.5-3in) lengths of root that carry a growing bud. It is easy to see the growing buds on the roots of mint.

This method is equally applicable for all the varieties mentioned above as suitable for root propagation, with the exception of Comfrey and Horseradish, where one simply slices the root into sections, 4-8cm (1½-3in) long, using a sharp knife to give a clean cut through the root. Do not worry, each will produce a plant!
   These cuttings lend themselves to being grown in plug trays.

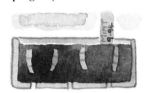

4 Make holes in the compost with a dibber. If using pots or seed trays these should be 3-6cm (1-2½in) apart. Plant the cutting vertically.

5 Cover the container with a small amount of compost, followed by a layer of Perlite level with the top of the container.

6 Label and date. This is most important because you cannot see what is in the container until the plant begins to grow and it is all too easy to forget what you have planted.

7 Average rooting time 2-3 weeks. Do not water until roots or top growth appears. Then apply liquid feed.

8 Slowly harden off the cuttings when rooted.

9 Pot on in a potting compost once they are weaned. Label and water well after transplanting. You can miss this stage out if you have grown the root cuttings in plug trays.

10 About 2-3 weeks after transplanting, when you can see that the plant is growing away, pinch out the top centre of the young cutting. This will encourage the plant to bush out, making it stronger as well as fuller.

11 Allow to grow on until a good-size root ball can be seen in the pot. Plant out in the garden when the last frosts are over.

LAYERING

If cuttings are difficult to root you can try layering, a process that encourages sections of plant to root while still attached to the parent. Bay, Rosemary, Sage are good examples of plants that suit this method.

1 Prune some low branches off the parent plant during the winter season to induce vigorous growth and cultivate the soil around the plant during winter and early spring by adding peat and grit to it.

2 Trim the leaves and side shoots of a young vigorous stem for 10-60cm (4-24in) below its growing tip.

3 Bring the stem down to ground level and mark its position on the soil. Dig a trench at that point, making one vertical side 10-15cm (4-6in) deep, and the other sloping towards the plant.

4 Roughen the stem at the point where it will touch the ground.

5 Peg it down into the trench against the straight side, then bend the stem at right angles behind the growing tip, so that it protrudes vertically. Then return the soil to the trench to bury the stem. Firm in well.

6 Water well using a watering can and keep the soil moist, especially in dry periods.

7 Sever the layering stem from its parent plant in autumn if well rooted, and 3-4 weeks later nip out the growing tip from the rooted layer to make plant bush out.

8 Check carefully that the roots have become well established before lifting the layered stem. If necessary, leave for a further year.

9 Replant either in the open ground or in a pot using the bark, grit, peat mix of compost. Label and leave to establish.

Mound Layering
A method similar to layering that not only creates new growth but also improves the appearance of old plants. This is particularly suitable for sages and thymes, which can woody in the centre.

1 In the spring, pile soil mixed with peat and sand over the bare woody centre until only young shoots show.

2 By late summer, roots will have formed on many of these shoots. They can be taken and planted in new locations as cuttings or by root division.

3 The old plant can then be dug up and disposed of.

HERB GARDENS

The gardens I have designed can be followed religiously, or adapted to meet your personal tastes, needs and of course space. It is with this last requirement in mind that I have specifically now put the exact size into the design and concentrated on the shape, layout and the relationship between plants. I hope these plans give you freedom of thought and some inspiration.

FIRST HERB GARDEN

When planning your first herb garden, choose plants that you will use and enjoy. I have designed this garden in exactly the same way as the one at my herb farm. Much as I would love to have a rambling herb garden, I need something practical and easy to manage, because the nursery plants need all my attention.

It is also important that the herbs are easy to get at, so that I can use it every day. By dividing the garden up into four sections and putting paving stones round the outside and through the middle, it is easy to maintain and provides good accessibility.

For this garden, I have chosen a cross-section of herbs with a bias towards culinary use, because the more you use and handle the plants, the more you will understand their habits. There is much contradictory advice on which herb to plant with which but many of these are old wives tales.

There are only a few warnings I will give: Do not plant dill and fennel together because they intermarry and become fendill, losing their unique flavours in the process. Equally, do not plant dill or coriander near wormwood as it will impair their flavour. Also, different mints near each other cross-pollinate and over the years will lose their individual identity. Finally, if you plan to collect the seed from lavenders, keep the species well apart.

Aside from that, if you like it, plant it.

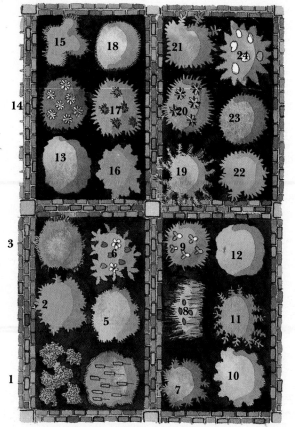

1   **Parsley** *Petroselinum crispum*
2   **Mint Pineapple** *Mentha suaveolens* 'Variegata'
3   **Fennel** *Foeniculum vulgare*
4   **Lavander Munstead** *Lavandula angustifolia* 'Munstead'
5   **Oregano Greek** *Origanum vulgare spp*
6   **Strawberry Alpine** *Fragaria vesca*
7   **Sage Purple** *Salvia officinalis* 'Purpurascens' *Group*
8   **Chives** *Allium schoenoprasum*
9   **Heartsease** *Viola tricolor*
10 **Marjoram Golden Curly** *Origanum vulgare* 'Aureum Crispum'
11 **Salad Burnet** *Sanguisorba minor*
12 **Thyme Lemon** *Thymus x citriodorus*
13 **Thyme Garden** *Thymus vulgaris*
14 **Chamomile Roman** *Chamaemelum nobile*
15 **Hyssop Rock** *Hyssopus offinialis ssp aristatus*
16 **Sorrel Buckler Leaf** *Rumex scutatus*
17 **Bergamot** *Monarda didyma*
18 **Curry, Dartington** *Helichrysum italicum* 'Dartington'
19 **Rosemary** *Rosmarinus officinalis*
20 **Borage** *Borago officinalis*
21 **Lemon Balm Variegated** *Melissa officinalis* 'Aurea'
22 **Mint Apple** *Mentha suaveolens*
23 **Winter Savory** *Satureja montana*
24 **Chervil** *Anthriscus cerefolium*

WHITE HERB GARDEN

This garden gave me great pleasure to create. For me, it is a herb garden with a different perspective.

It has a row of steps going from the road to the front door of the house. Either side of the steps is a dwarf white lavender hedge. In spring before the lavender, and just before the lily of the valley, are in flower, the sweet woodruff gives a carpet of small white flowers. This is the start of the white garden, which then flowers throughout the year through to autumn. It is a most attractive garden with a mixture of scents, foliage and flowers.

This planting combination can easily be adapted to suit a border. Even though it is not a conventional herb garden, all the herbs can be used in their traditional way. The garlic chives with baked potatoes, the horehound for coughs, the chamomile to make a soothing tea, and the lavender to make lavender bags or to use in the bath.

The great thing about a garden like this is that it requires very little work to maintain. The hedge is the only part that needs attention – trim in the spring and after flowering in order to maintain its shape.

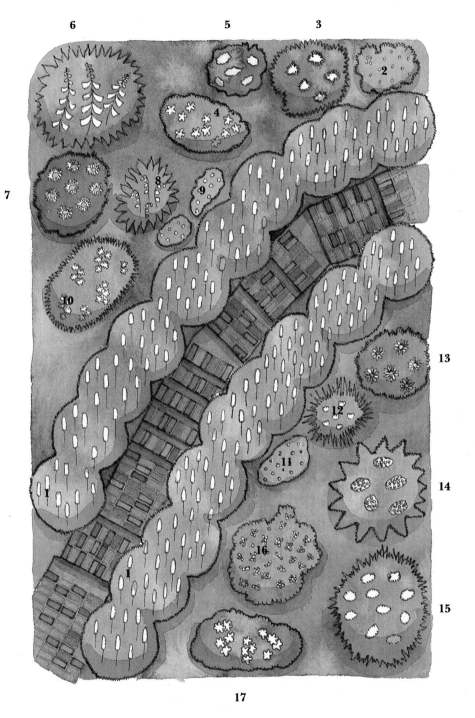

1	**Lavender White (dwarf)** *Lavandula angustifolia nana alba*	
2	**Sweet Woodruff** *Galium odoratum*	
3	**Bergamot Snow Maiden** *Monarda punctata* 'Schneewittchen'	
4	**Jacob's Ladder (white)** *Polemonium caeruleum album*	
5	**Yarrow** *Achillea millefolium*	
6	**Foxgloves (white)** *Digitalis purpurea alba* (POISONOUS)	
7	**Chamomile Roman** *Chamaemelum nobile*	
8	**Lily of the Valley** *Convallaria majalis* (POISONOUS)	
9	**Thyme White** *Thymus serpyllum albus*	
10	**Hyssop White** *Hyssopus officinalis albus*	
11	**Thyme Snowdrift** *Thymus serpyllum* 'Snowdrift'	
12	**Chives Garlic** *Allium tuberosum*	
13	**Pyrethrum** *Tanacetum cinerariifolium*	
14	**Sweet Cicely** *Myrrhis odorata*	
15	**Valerian** *Valeriana officinalis*	
16	**Horehound** *Marrubium vulgare*	
17	**Prostanthera** *Prostanthera cuneata*	

HERBS IN CONTAINERS

In all the years I have been growing herbs I have only found a very very few that cannot be grown in containers. In the A-Z section of this book I have given details not only about each herb and what size container best suits it, but also where to place it. This section provides more general information and advice on container growing that is applicable to most herbs.

CONTAINERS

* Choose the container to suit the plant. If it is a tall plant make sure the container has a base wide enough to prevent it toppling over, even if placed outside in a high wind.

* A collection of containers is sometimes much easier to look after than a window box, and you can give each herb its own individual bit of tender loving care.

* If using unconventional containers – old watering cans, sinks, a half beer barrel – make sure they have drainage holes, and gravel or broken pots in the bottom of the container to stop the holes clogging up.

HANGING BASKETS

Herbs can suit hanging baskets, but the position is crucial. They dislike high wind and full sun all day. Also, they are mostly fast growers and if too cramped or over- or under-watered they will drop their leaves. They also benefit from being picked regularly, which is not always possible in a hanging basket.

I can recommend the following: double flowered chamomile, creeping thymes, prostrate rosemary, catmint, creeping savory, golden marjoram, dwarf marjoram, pineapple mint, pennyroyal, and maiden pinks – to name but a few. Other candidates can be found in the A to Z section.

Preparation of Hanging Baskets
* Line the basket with sphagnum moss followed by a layer of black plastic with holes punched in it.

* Fill the basket half full with compost. Position the plants, trailers at the side, taller, more upright herbs in the middle. Do not overcrowd.

*Fill up with compost. Water in well. Let it drain before hanging.

* Check hanging position for accessibility. In the height of the season you will need to water at least night and morning. Make sure, too, that it cannot fall on anyone's head.

COMPOSTS AND ORGANIC FERTILIZER

Choosing the right compost is essential for healthy plants.

Own Mix Bark, Peat, Grit
You will have realized that I generally use the bark, peat, grit mix of compost. I have found this reliable: the open mix helps prevent over-watering; the bark retains water, which protects against under-watering and keeps the compost open to help absorb water if ever it dries out completely. It is suitable for containers and hanging baskets alike. Another plus is that you know what nutrients are in it, so will be able to feed in a balanced way.

Own Soil-based Mix
If you wish to make a soil-based compost of your own this recipe is fairly reliable.

4 parts good weed-free garden top soil
3 parts well-rotted garden compost
3 parts moist peat
1 part horticultural sharp sand

Multipurpose Potting Compost
This is usually peat based with added chemicals. Bags can be bought in numerous outlets, from garden centres to supermarkets. The bags are light and the compost is clean and easy to use. On the negative side, you will need to feed regularly as nutrients are soon depleted; also the compost is light, so watch out that large plants do not fall over. The most frequent problem is that it takes up water poorly if ever it dries out.

Fertilizer
You can buy organic fertilizer from garden centres and hardware shops. The following organic fertilizers are ideal to be added to potting or seed sowing composts when planting up.

Liquid seaweed
This contains small amounts of nitrogen, phosphorous, potassium, and it is also rich in trace elements. It not only makes a good soil feed but as the elements are easily taken in by the plant, it can also be sprayed on as a foliar feed.

Calcified Seaweed
This contains calcium, magnesium, sodium and numerous trace elements. It is ideal for adding to seed compost. Add according to the manufacturer's instructions.

Alternative Composts
Here are some alternative composts that can be used for container growing.

John Innes
This can be purchased in any garden centre or hardware store. It is soil-based and includes chemicals. On the plus side, it stays richer in nutrients longer, making feeding less critical; it holds water well and is a stable compost for a large plant. If it does dry out, it takes up water easily. The major watch point is that it is easy to over-water.

There are usually 3 different grades of compost, though some manufacturers combine No.1 and No.2. No.1 is for growing rooted cuttings, No.2 for seedlings and No.3 for final potting. The numbers indicate the amount of nutrients. You must choose the correct one for the job. One word of warning - this is not a good compost for hanging baskets, because it is heavy when wet.

Peat-free Composts
These are becoming more readily available as we become aware of the need to conserve our diminishing peat fields. They are made of the following:

Coir

This is a by-product of coconuts. Because it is very fashionable there are quite a few product varieties on the market (at a marked-up price), some more reliable than others. I could argue that it takes a lot of natural resources to ship them from their mountain homes half way round the world, but I won't labour that.

In itself coir is worth looking at, although it does not readily decompose and water zooms through it. For this reason some manufacturers are introducing a jelly that retains water, releasing it gradually. Coir compost is light, so there may be a stability problem with tall or large plants. A final minus point – the nutrients are soon depleted so you will need to feed from the start.

Composted Bark

These composts are now becoming widely available. Although they are fine for propagating under mist, I personally do not recommend them for container growing if used straight, with no peat or soil. Watering and nutrient loss are the two major problems. Also, if the bark has not been composted for long enough, it can leach the nutrients and starve the plants. However, mixed with peat or soil, bark is a great asset.

MAINTENANCE

Spring: This is the time of year to pot on plants if necessary. A good sign of when they need this is that the roots are truly protruding from the bottom of the container. Use a pot next size up. Carefully remove the plant from its old pot. Give it a good tidy up – remove any weed, dead leaves. If it is a perennial, trim the growing tip to promote new bushy growth. Place gravel or other drainage material in the bottom of the container and keep the compost sweet by adding a tablespoon full of granulated charcoal. As soon as the plant starts producing new growth or flowers, start feeding regularly with liquid seaweed.

Summer: Keep a careful eye on the watering; make sure the pots do not dry out fully. Move some plants out of the midday sun. Dead head any flowers. Feed with liquid seaweed, on average once a week. Remove any pest-damaged leaves.

Autumn: Cut back the perennial herbs. Weed containers and at the same time remove some of the top compost and re-dress. Bring any tender plants inside before the frosts. Start reducing the watering.

Winter: Protect all container-grown plants from frosts. If possible move into a cold greenhouse, conservatory or garage. If the weather is very severe cover the containers in a layer of sacking. Keep watering to the absolute minimum.

Back row, left to right: **Lungwort,** *Pulmonaria officinalis, Prostanthera rotundifolia,* **Variegated Box,** *Buxus sempervirens* 'Elegantissimus', **Rosemary Benenden Blue,** *Rosmarinus officinalis* 'Benenden Blue', **Box,** *Buxus sempervirens;* front row, left to right: *Prostanthera rotundifolia rosea,* **Marjoram Golden Curly,** *Origanum vulgare* 'Aureum', **Rue Jackman's Blue,** *Ruta Graveolens* 'Jackman's Blue', **Old Warrior** *Artemisia pontica*

Harvesting

The more you pick the healthier the plant. People are told that if their chives start to flower they will have no more fresh leaves until the following year. Rubbish! Pick some of the flowers to use in salads and, if the plant is then cut back to within 4cm (1½in) of the ground and given a good feed of liquid fertilizer, it will produce another crop of succulent leaves within a month. Keep two chive plants: one for flowering and one for harvesting.

Herbs can be harvested from very early on in their growing season. This encourages the plant to produce vigorous new growth. It allows the plant to be controlled both in shape and size. Most herbs reach their peak of flavour just before they flower. Snip off suitable stems early in the day before the sun is fully up, or even better on a cloudy day (provided it is not too humid). Cut whole stems rather than single leaves or flowers. Always use a sharp knife, sharp scissors or secateurs, and cut lengths of 5–8cm (2–3in) from the tip of the branch, this being the new soft growth. Do not cut into any of the older, woody growth. Cut from all over the plant, leaving it looking shapely. Pick herbs which are clean and free from pests and disease; they should not be discoloured or damaged in any way. If herbs are covered in garden soil, sponge them quickly and lightly with cold water, not hot as this will draw out the oils prematurely. Pat dry as quickly as possible. Keep each species separately so that they do not contaminate each other. Do not be greedy!

Harvesting

Annual herbs
Most can be harvested at least twice during a growing season. Cut them to within 10–15cm (4–6in) of the ground, and feed with liquid fertilizer after each cutting. Do not cut the plants too low in the first harvesting as they will not be able to recover in time to give a further cutting later on. Give annuals their final cut of the season before the first frosts; they will have stopped growing some weeks before.

Perennial herbs
In the first year of planting, perennials will give one good crop; thereafter it will be possible to harvest two or three times during the growing season. Do not cut into the woody growth unless deliberately trying to prevent growth; again, cut well before frosts as cutting late in the season may weaken plants and inhibit them from surviving the winter. There are of course exceptions; sage is still very good after frosts, and both thyme and golden marjoram (with some protection) can be picked gently even in mid-winter.

Flowers and seeds
Pick flowers for drying when they are barely opened. Seed should be collected as soon as you notice a change in colour of the seed pod; if when you tap the pod a few scatter on the ground, it is the time to gather them. Seeds ripen very fast, so watch them carefully.

Roots
These are at their peak of flavour when they have completed a growing season. Dig them through autumn as growth ceases. Lift whole roots with a garden fork, taking care not to puncture or bruise the outer skin. Wash them free of soil. Cut away any remains of top growth and any fibrous off-shoots. For drying cut large, thick roots in half length-ways and then into smaller pieces for ease.

Individual herbs laid out for drying

Drying

The object of drying herbs is to eliminate the water content of the plant quickly and, at the same time, to retain the essential oils. It looks pretty to have bunches of herbs hanging up in a kitchen but most of the flavour will be lost quickly. Herbs need to be dried in a warm, dark, dry and well-ventilated place. The faster they dry, the better retained are the aromatic oils. Darkness helps to prevent loss of colour and unique flavours. The area must be dry, with a good air flow, to hasten the drying process and to discourage mould.

Suitable places for drying herbs include:
* an airing cupboard

* attic space immediately under the roof (provided it does not get too hot)
* in the oven at low temperature and with the door ajar (place the herbs on a brown piece of paper with holes punched in it and check regularly that the herbs are not over-heating
* a plate-warming compartment
* a spare room with curtains shut and door open.

The temperature should be maintained at slightly below body temperature, between 21–33°C/70–90°F.

Herbs should always be dried separately from each other, especially the stronger scented ones like lovage. Spread them in a single layer on trays or slatted wooden racks covered with muslin or netting. The trays or frames should be placed in the drying areas so that they have good air circulation. Herbs need to be turned over by hand several times during the first two days.

Roots require a higher temperature – from 50–60°C/120–140°F. They are quicker and easier to dry in an oven and require regular turning until they are fragile and break easily. Specific requirements are given for each herb in the A–Z section.

Seed should be dried without any artificial heat and in an airy place. Almost-ripe seed heads can be hung in paper bags (plastic causes them to sweat) so the majority of seeds will fall into the bag as they mature. They need to be dried thoroughly before storing and the process can take up to two weeks.

TIP: An alternative method for flowers, roots or seed heads is to tie them in small bundles of 8 to 10 stems. Do not pack the stems too tightly together, as air needs to circulate through and around the bunches. Then hang them on coat-hangers in an airy, dark room until they are dry.

The length of drying time varies from herb to herb, and week to week. The determining factor is the state of the plant material. If herbs are stored before drying is complete, moisture will be reabsorbed from the atmosphere and the herb will soon deteriorate. Leaves should be both brittle and crisp. They should break easily into small pieces but should not reduce to a powder when touched. The roots should be brittle and dry right through. Any softness or sponginess means they are not sufficiently dry and, if stored that way, will rot.

A Quick Method of Herb Drying

Microwave manufacturers have said it takes 3 to 4 minutes to dry thoroughly 10 sprigs of any herb! I have tried. It is easy to over-dry and cook the leaves to the point of complete disintegration. I have found that small-leafed herbs such as rosemary and thyme take about 1 minute, whilst the larger, moist leaves of mint dry in about 3 minutes. Add an eggcupful of water to the microwave during the process. **And be warned! Sage can ignite . . .**

Storing

Herbs lose their flavour and colour if not stored properly. Pack the leaves or roots, not too tightly, into a dark glass jar with an air-tight screw top. Label with name and date. Keep in a dark cupboard; nothing destroys the quality of the herb quicker at this stage than exposure to light.
After the initial storing, keep a check on the jars for several days. If moisture

Parsley stored in a bag for freezing, together with ice cubes for convenience

starts to form on the inside of the container, the herbs have not been dried correctly. Return them to the drying area and allow further drying time.

Most domestic herb requirements are comparatively small so there is little point in storing large amounts for a long time. The shelf life of dried herbs is only about 1 year so it is sufficient to keep enough just for the winter.

Dried herbs are usually 3 to 4 times more powerful than fresh. When a recipe calls for a tablespoon of a fresh herb and you only have dried use a teaspoonful.

TIP: If you have large dark jars, thyme and rosemary can be left on the stalk. This makes it easier to use them in casseroles and stews and to remove before serving.

Freezing Herbs

Freezing is great for culinary herbs as colour, flavour and the nutritional value of the fresh young leaves are retained. It is becoming an increasingly popular way to preserve and store culinary herbs, being quick and easy. I believe it is far better to freeze herbs such as fennel, dill,, parsley, tarragon and chives than to dry them.

Pick the herbs and, if necessary, rinse with cold water, and shake dry before freezing, being careful not to bruise the leaves. Put small amounts of herbs into labelled, plastic bags, either singly, or as a mixture for bouquet garnis. Either have a set place in the freezer for them or put the bags into a container, so that they do not get damaged with the day-to-day use of the freezer.

There is no need to thaw herbs before use; simply add them to the cooking as required. For chopped parsley, freeze the bunches whole in bags and, when you remove them from the freezer, crush the parsley in its bag with your hand. Do not be distracted in this task or you will have a herb that has thawed and is a limp piece of greenery. This technique is good for all fine-leaved herbs.

Another way to freeze herbs conveniently is to put finely-chopped leaves into an ice-cube tray and top them up with water. The average cube holds 1 tablespoon chopped herbs and 1 teaspoon water.

TIP: The flowers of borage and the leaves of the variegated mints look very attractive when frozen individually in ice-cubes for drinks or fruit salads.

Agastache foeniculum

ANISE HYSSOP

Also known as Giant Hyssop, Anise Hyssop, Blue Giant Hyssop, Fennel Hyssop, Fragrant Giant Hyssop. From the family Labiatae.

Anise hyssop is a native of North America, The Mosquito Plant and *A. mexicana* '*Brittonastrum mexicana*' of Mexico, and *A. rugosa* of Korea.

There are few references to the history of this lovely herb. According to Allen Paterson, Director of the Royal Botanical Garden in Ontario, it is a close cousin of the Bergamots. It is common in North American herb gardens and is certainly worth including in any herb garden for its flowers and scent. The long spikes of purple, blue and pink flowers are big attractions for bees and butterflies.

SPECIES

Agastache cana
The Mosquito Plant
Half-hardy perennial. Ht 60cm (2ft), spread 30cm (1ft). Pink tubular flowers in the summer with aromatic oval mid-green toothed leaves.

Agastache mexicana
'Brittonastrum mexicana'
(or 'Cedronella mexican')
Half-hardy perennial. Ht 1m (3ft), spread 30cm (1ft). Whorls of small tubular summer-time flowers in shades from pink to crimson. Leaves oval pointed, toothed and mid-green with an eucalyptus scent.

Agastache rugosa
Korean Mint
Hardy perennial. Ht 1m (3ft), spread 30cm (1ft). Lovely mauve/purple flower spikes in summer. Distinctly minty scented mid-green oval pointed leaves.

Anise Hyssop
Agastache foeniculum

Agastache foeniculum
Anise Hyssop
Hardy perennial. Ht 60cm (2ft), spread 30cm (1ft). Long purple flower spikes in summer. Aniseed scented mid-green oval leaves.

CONTAINER GROWING

Not suitable for growing indoors. However, anise hyssop and Korean mint both make good patio plants provided the container is at least 25-30cm (10-12in) diameter. Use the bark, peat mix of compost, and a liquid fertilizer feed only once a year after flowering. If you feed the plant beforehand, the flowers will be poor. Keep well watered in summer.

CULTIVATION

Propagation

Note: *A. mexicana* can only be propagated by cuttings.

Seed

The small fine seeds need warmth to germinate: 17°C (65°F). Use the cardboard method and artificial heating if sowing in early spring.

Use either prepared seed or plug trays or if you have only a few seeds directly into a pot and cover with Perlite. Germination takes 10–20 days.

One can also sow outside in the autumn when the soil is warm, but the young plants will need protection throughout the winter months.

When the seedlings are large enough to handle prick out and pot on using a bark or peat mix of compost. In mid-spring, when air and soil temperature has risen, plant out at a distance of 45cm (18in).

Cuttings

Take cuttings of soft young shoots in spring; when all the species root well. Use 50per cent bark, 50per cent peat mix of compost. After a full period of weaning cuttings should be strong enough to plant out in the early autumn.

Semi-ripe wood cuttings may be taken in late summer, use the same compost mix. After they have rooted, pot up, and winter in a cold frame or cold greenhouse.

Division

This is a good alternative way to maintain a short-lived perennial. In the second or third year divide the creeping roots either by the 'forks back-to-back' method, or by digging up the whole plant and dividing.

Pests and Diseases

Being an aromatic plant, pests keep their distance. Rarely suffers from disease, although seedlings can damp off.

Maintenance

Spring: Sow seeds.
Summer: Take softwood or semi-ripe cuttings late season.
Autumn: Tidy up the plants by cutting back the old flower heads and woody growth. Sow seeds. Protect young plants from frost.
Winter: Protect half-hardy species (and Anise hyssop below –6°C (20°F)) with either agricultural fleece, bark or straw.

Garden Cultivation

All species like a rich, moist soil and full sun, and will adapt very well to most ordinary soils if planted in a sunny situation. All are short lived and should be propagated each year to ensure continuity.

Anise hyssop, although hardier than the other species, still needs protection below –6°C (20°F).

The Mexican half-hardy species need protection below –3°C (26°F).

Harvest

Flowers

Cut for drying just as they begin to open.

Leaves

Cut leaves just before late spring flowering.

Seeds

Heads turn brown as the seed ripens. At the first sign of the seed falling, pick and hang upside down with a paper bag tied over the heads.

OTHER USES

Anise Hyssop, Korean Mint and *Agastache mexicana* all have scented leaves which makes them suitable for potpourris.

Summer fruit cup made with anise hyssop

CULINARY

The two varieties most suitable are –

Anise Hyssop

Leaves can be used in salads and to make refreshing tea. Like borage, they can be added to summer fruit cups. Equally they can be chopped and used as a seasoning in pork dishes or in savory rice.

Flowers can be added to fruit salads and cups giving a lovely splash of colour.

Korean Mint

Leaves have a strong peppermint flavour and make a very refreshing tea, said to be good first thing in the morning after a night on the town. They are also good chopped up in salads, and the flowers look very attractive scattered over a pasta salad.

Korean mint tea

Alchemilla

LADY'S MANTLE

From the family Rosaceae.

Lady's mantle is a native of the mountains of Europe, Asia and America. It is found not only in damp places but also in dry shady woods.

The Arab 'alkemelych' (alchemy) was thought to be the source of the herb's Latin generic name, *Alchemilla*. The crystal dew lying in perfect pearl drops on the leaves have long inspired poets and alchemists, and was reputed to have healing and magical properties, even to preserve a woman's youth provided she collected the dew in May, alone, in full moonlight, naked, and with bare feet as a sign of purity and to ward off any lurking forces.

In the medieval period it was dedicated to the Virgin Mary, hence Lady's Mantle was considered a woman's protector, and nicknamed 'a woman's best friend', and was used not only to regulate the menstrual cycle and to ease the effects of menopause, but also to reduce inflammation of the female organs. In the 18th century, women applied the leaves to their breasts to make them recover shape after they had been swelled with milk.

It is still prescribed by herbalists today.

Lady's Mantle *Alchemilla mollis*

Alchemilla conjuncta
Lady's Mantle Conjuncta
Hardy perennial. Ht 30cm (12in), spread 30cm (12in) or more. Tiny, greenish-yellow flowers in summer. Leaves star-shaped, bright green on top with lovely silky silver hairs underneath. An attractive plant suitable for ground cover, rockeries and dry banks.

SPECIES

Alchemilla alpine
Alpine Lady's Mantle
Known in America as Silvery Lady's Mantle.
Hardy perennial. Ht 15cm (6in), spread 60cm (24in) or more. Tiny, greenish-yellow flowers in summer. Leaves rounded, lobed, pale green and covered in silky hairs. An attractive plant suitable for ground cover, rockeries and dry banks.

Alchemilla mollis
Lady's Mantle (Garden variety)
Hardy perennial. Ht and spread 50cm (20in). Tiny, greenish-yellow flowers in summer. Large, pale green, rounded leaves with crinkled edges.

Alchemilla xanthochlora (vulgaris)
Lady's Mantle (Wild flower variety)
Also known as Lion's Foot, Bear's Foot and Nine Hooks.

Hardy perennial. Ht 15-45cm (6-18in), spread 50cm (20in). Tiny, bright greenish/yellow flowers in summer. Round, pale green leaves with crinkled edges.

CULTIVATION

Propagation
Seed

Why is it that something that self-seeds readily around the garden can be so difficult to raise from seed? Sow its very fine seed in early spring or autumn into prepared seed or plug trays (use the cardboard method), and cover with Perlite. No bottom heat required. Germination can either be sparse or prolific, taking 2-3 weeks. If germinating in the autumn, winter seedlings in the trays and plant out the following spring when the frosts are over, at a distance of 45cm (18in) apart.

Division

All established plants can be divided in the spring or autumn. Replant in the garden where desired.

Pests and Diseases
This plant rarely suffers from pests or disease.

Maintenance
Spring: Divide established plants. Sow seeds if necessary.
Summer: To prevent self-seeding, cut off flowerheads as they begin to die back.
Autumn: Divide established plants if necessary. Sow seed.
Winter: No need for protection.

Garden Cultivation
This fully hardy plant grows in all but boggy soils, in sun or partial shade. Seed can be sown in spring where you want the plant to flower. Thin the seedlings to 30cm (12in) apart.

  This is a most attractive garden plant in borders or as an edging plant, but it can become a bit of a nuisance, seeding everywhere. To prevent this, cut back after flowering and at the same time cut back old growth.

Early morning dew on
Alchemilla mollis

Harvest
Cut young leaves after the dew has dried for use throughout the summer. Harvest for drying as plant comes into flower.

CONTAINER GROWING

All forms of Lady's Mantle adapt to container growing and look very pretty indeed. Use a soil-based compost, water throughout the summer, but feed with liquid fertilizer (following manufacturer's instructions) only occasionally. In the winter, when the plant dies back, put the container in a cold greenhouse or cold frame, and water only very occasionally. Lady's Mantle can be grown in hanging baskets as a centre piece.

MEDICINAL

Used by herbalists for menstrual disorders. It has been said that if you drink an infusion of green parts of the plant for 10 days each month it will help relieve menopausal discomfort. It can also be used as a mouth rinse after tooth extraction. Traditionally, the alpine species has been considered more effective, although this is not proven.

Leaves laid out for drying

CULINARY

Tear young leaves, with their mild bitter taste, into small pieces and toss into salads. Many years ago Marks & Spencer had a yoghurt made with Lady's Mantle leaves! I wish I had tried it.

OTHER USES
Excellent for flower arranging.
  Leaves can be boiled for green wool dye and are used in veterinary medicine for the treatment of diarrhoea.

Calendula officinalis

MARIGOLD

Also known as Souci, Marybud, Bulls Eye, Garden Marigold, Holligold, Marybud, Pot Marigold and Common Marigold. From the family Compositae.

Native of Mediterranean and Iran. Distributed throughout the world as a garden plant.

This sunny little flower – the 'merrybuds' of Shakespeare – was first used in Indian and Arabic cultures, before being 'discovered' by the ancient Egyptians and Greeks.

The Egyptians valued the marigold as a rejuvenating herb, and the Greeks garnished and flavoured food with its golden petals. The botanical name comes from the Latin 'calendae', meaning the first day of the month.

In India wreaths of marigold were used to crown the gods and goddesses. In medieval times they were considered an emblem of love and used as chief ingredient in a complicated spell that promised young maidens knowledge of whom they would marry. To dream of them was a sign of all good things; simply to look at them would drive away evil humours.

In the American Civil War, marigold leaves were used by the doctors on the battlefield to treat open wounds.

SPECIES

Calendula officinalis
Marigold
Hardy annual. Ht and spread 60cm (24in). Daisy-like, single or double flowers, yellow or orange: from spring to autumn. Light green, aromatic, lance-shaped leaves.

Marigold
Calendula officinalis

CULTIVATION

Propagation
Seeds
Seeds can be sown in the autumn under protection directly into prepared pots or singly into plug trays, covering lightly with compost. They can be wintered in these containers and planted out in the spring after any frost, 30-45cm (12-18in) apart.

Pests and Diseases
Slugs love the leaves of young marigolds. Keep

night-time vigil with a torch and a bucket, or lay beer traps. In the latter part of the season, plants can become infested with blackfly. Treat this in the early stages by brushing off the fly and cutting away the affected areas, or later on by spraying with a horticultural soap. Very late in the season, the leaves sometimes become covered with a powdery mildew. Cut off those affected and burn them in case it spreads.

Maintenance
Spring: Sow seeds in garden.
Summer: Dead head flowers to promote more flowering.
Autumn: Sow seeds under protection for early spring flowering.
Winter: Protect young plants.

Garden Cultivation
Marigold is a very tolerant plant, growing in any soil that is not waterlogged, but prefers, and looks best in, a sunny position.

The flowers are sensitive to variations of temperature and dampness. Open flowers forecast a fine day. Encourage continuous flowering by dead heading. It self-seeds abundantly but seems never to become a nuisance. Self-sown seeds normally germinate in autumn and overwinter successfully if temperatures do not go persistently below 0°C (32°F). They will flower the following summer.

Do not confuse the pot marigold, *Calendula officinalis,* with the French or African marigolds, which are *Tagetes.*

Marigolds attract whitefly away from other plants.

Harvest
Pick flowers just as they open during summer, both for fresh use and for drying. Dry at a low temperature. You can make a colourful oil.

Pick leaves young for fresh use; they are not much good preserved.

CULINARY

Flower petals make a very good culinary dye. They have been used for butter and cheese, and as a poor man's saffron to colour rice. They are also lovely in salads and omelettes, and make an interesting cup of tea.

Young leaves can be added to salads.

Sweet Marigold Buns
Makes 18

100g/4oz softened butter
100g/4oz caster sugar
2 eggs, size 1 or 2
100g/4oz self-raising flour
1 teaspoon baking powder
2 tablespoons fresh marigold petals

Put the butter, sugar, eggs, sifted flour and baking powder into bowl, and mix together until smooth and glossy. Fold in 1½ tablespoons of marigold petals. Turn the mixture into greased bun tins or individual paper cake cases. Sprinkle a few petals onto each bun with a little sugar. Bake in an oven 160°C/325°F/Gas Mark 3 for approximately 25-30 minutes.

CONTAINER GROWING

Marigolds look very cheerful in containers and combine well with other plants. Well suited to window boxes, but not so in hanging baskets, where they will become stretched and leggy.

Use the bark, peat compost. Pinch out the growing tips to stop the plant from becoming too tall and leggy. Dead head flowers to encourage more blooms.

OTHER USES
There are many skin and cosmetic preparations that contain marigold. Infuse the flowers and use as a skin lotion to reduce large pores, nourish and clear the skin, and clear up spots and pimples.

MEDICINAL

Marigold flowers contain antiseptic, anti-fungal and anti-bacterial properties that promote healing. Make a compress or poultice of the flowers for burns, scalds, or stings. Also useful in the treatment of varicose veins, chilblains and impetigo. A cold infusion may be used as an eyewash for conjunctivitis, and can be a help in the treatment of thrush.

The sap from the stem has a reputation for removing warts, corns and calluses.

Marigold skin lotion

Dianthus

PINKS

Also known as Clove Pink and Gillyflower.
From the family Caryophyllaceae.

The true pinks are derived from *Dianthus plumarius,* a native of Eastern Europe and introduced to Britain in the 17th century. From then on, numerous varieties have been cultivated. The wild forefather of the carnation, *Dianthus caryophyllus,* it is a native of Central and Southern Europe; both species and their varieties are now cultivated throughout the world.

Dianthus comes from the words 'dios', meaning divine, and 'anthos', meaning flower, and was coined by Theophrastus, a Greek botanist who lived in 370-285 BC, alluding to their fragrance and neatness of flower. Both the Romans and Greeks gave pinks a place of honour and made coronets and garlands from the flowers. The strong sweet clove scent has made it popular for both culinary and perfumery purposes for more than 2,000 years. In the 17th century it was recognized that the flowers could be crystallized, and the petals were used in soups, sauces, cordials and wine, and infused in vinegar.

The Cheddar Pink, Cleeve Pink or Cliff Pink, was discovered early in the 18th century by Wiltshire botanist, Samuel Brewer. It became as famous as Cheddar cheese and is mentioned in all the guide books.

SPECIES

Dianthus armaria
Deptford Pink
Evergreen hardy perennial. Ht 30-45cm (12-18in), spread 45cm (18in). Small bunches of little, cerise or pink, unscented flowers in summer. In dull weather the flower closes. Lance-shaped, narrow, dark green leaves.
This is a wild plant and is becoming increasingly rare. It looks most attractive growing in a border.

Dianthus caryophyllus
Carnation
Evergreen hardy perennial. Ht 45-60cm (18-24in), spread 45cm (18in). Rose or purply pink flowers, having a spicy sweet scent. Loose mats of narrow, grey/green, lance-shaped leaves.

Dianthus deltoides
Maiden Pink
Evergreen hardy perennial. Ht 15cm (6in), spread 30cm (12in). Small cerise, pink or white flowers are borne singly all summer. Small, narrow, lance-shaped, dark green leaves.
Maiden pinks are a lovely spreading plant for rock gardens or gravelly paths.

Dianthus gratianopolitanus syn. Dianthus caesius
Cheddar Pink
Evergreen hardy perennial. Ht 15cm (6in), spread 30cm (12in). Very fragrant, rich pink to magenta, flat flowers are borne singly all summer. Loose mats of narrow, grey/green, lance-shaped leaves.
The Cheddar pink is very rare and a protected species in Britain, but is more common in Europe.

Dianthus plumarius
Pinks
Evergreen hardy perennial. Ht 15cm (6in), spread 30cm (12in). Very fragrant white flowers with dark crimson centres borne singly all summer. Loose mats of narrow, grey/green, lance-shaped leaves.
These are related to the Cheddar pink and are the origin of the Garden pink.

Some old fashioned garden pinks worth looking for:

Dianthus 'Gran's Favourite'
Fragrant semi-double white flowers with deep purple/red centre.

Dianthus 'London Delight'
Fragrant flowers are semi-double and coloured lavender laced with purple.

Dianthus 'Mrs Sinkins'
Heavily scented flower, fringed, fully double, and white.

Dianthus 'Prudence'
Fragrant semi-double flowers, pinkish-white with purple lacing. This variety has a spreading habit.

CULTIVATION

Propagation
Seed
Although pinks can be propagated by seed, they can turn out to be very variable in height, colour and habit. The named forms can only be propagated by cuttings or by layering.

Sow the small seed in the autumn when it is fresh, or in early spring, in prepared seed or plug trays; cover with Perlite. If sown in the autumn the young plants must be wintered under cover. It is critical not to over-water young plants or they will rot off. Allow plenty of air to flow through the greenhouse on warm days – if you open up the cold frame, close it at night. In the spring, when the seedlings are large enough to handle and after a period of hardening off, plant out in the garden about 30cm (1ft) apart.

Cuttings
Softwood cuttings can be taken in the spring. Alternatively heel cuttings can be taken in the early autumn (see step 6 of Softwood Cuttings, page 218), using the bark, peat, grit compost. Again, water the compost before taking the cuttings, then keep the compost on the drier side of moist, so helping to prevent disease.

Division
After flowering, the plants can be dug up and divided.

Layering
In late summer plants can be layered.

Pests and Diseases
The main pest is the red spider mite. Use a liquid horticultural soap and spray at first sign of the pest. Alternatively, introduce the natural predator **Phytoseiulus persimilis**, following the instructions that will accompany them. Do not use both.

The main disease appears at propagation stage, when the young plants can rot off, usually caused by a fungus attack, triggered off by the compost being too wet. Organically there is nothing one can use to get rid of this; the infected plants must be removed.

Maintenance
Spring: Sow seeds. Take stem cuttings.
Summer: Dead head flowers to prolong flowering. Divide after flowering. Layer plants.
Autumn: Take heal cuttings. Sow seed.
Winter: No need for protection.

Garden Cultivation
Pinks prefer a truly well-drained soil, short of plant nutrient, and a sunny, sheltered site.

They are happy by the sea or growing in a rock garden. With new varieties being developed all the time, many old pinks and carnations have been lost. But you can still find some excellent specialist nurseries that offer a great range.

Harvest
Pick flowers when they are open either to use fresh, or to crystallize the petals or to dry for potpourris or to use for oil or vinegar.

CONTAINER GROWING

All the above mentioned pinks are happy in containers, as long as their compost is free-draining; so use the bark, peat, grit mix. They combine well with other plants, and look just a bit special on their own. Maiden pinks look effective in hanging baskets.

Crystallized dianthus flowers

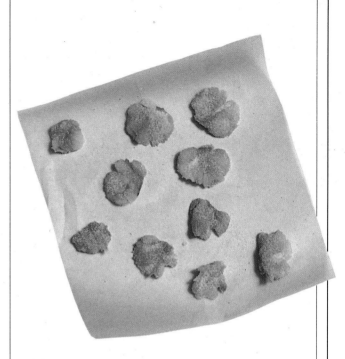

CULINARY

If you remove a petal from the flower you will notice that it has a white heel. This must be removed before the petals are added to any food as it is very bitter. Add petals to salads, and to fruit pies and sandwiches. Use to flavour sugar and jam, or to make a syrup. Add crystallized flower petals to cakes and decorate puddings.

Infuse the open flowers in almond oil for sweet oil or in wine vinegar for floral vinegar.

Dissected dianthus flowers showing the white heel

MEDICINAL

A tonic cordial can be made from the flower petals and is even better when combined with white wine! Makes an excellent nerve tonic.

OTHER USES

Add dried petals to potpourris, scented sachets, and cosmetic products.

Fragaria vesca

WILD STRAWBERRY

Also known as Mountain Strawberry, Wood Strawberry and Alpine Strawberry. From the family Rosaceae.

These delightful plants are found mainly in forests, clearings and shady roadsides in the cool temperate climates of Europe, northern Asia, Australia and North America.

Strawberry's name does not in fact originate from a traditional practice of placing straw beneath the berries to keep them clean. Rather, it dates back to the 10th century when the Anglo-Saxon word 'straw' meant small particles of chaff, and which in this case referred to the scattering of pips (achenes) over the surface of the fruit.

Fragaria originates from 'fraga', the old Latin name 'fragrans' meaning fragrant.

The fruit of this herb is dedicated to Venus and the Virgin Mary.

SPECIES

There are many forms of this small strawberry, some with variegated leaves, some with white fruit; the 2 identified here are the originals.

Fragaria vesca
Wild Strawberry
Hardy perennial. Ht 15-30cm (6-12in), spread 18 cm (7in), more if you include the runners. The flowers have 4 or 5 white petals with a yellow centre in spring to early summer. The leaf is composed of 3 brightish green leaflets with serrated edges.

Fragaria vesca sempiflorans
Alpine Strawberry
Hardy perennial. Ht 5-25cm (2-10in), spread 15cm (6in). The flowers have 4 or 5 white petals with a yellow centre from spring to autumn. The leaf is made of 3 brightish green leaflets with serrated edges. True Alpine strawberry does not set down runners, so propagate by seed only.

CULTIVATION

Propagation
Seed
The seed of the strawberry is imbedded all around the surface of the fruit. To collect it, leave the fruit in the summer sun until fully dry and shrivelled; then rub the seed off. Sow in late winter, early spring. Do not cover. A bottom heat of 15°C (60°F) is helpful. Germination will take place in a couple of weeks. Later in spring the seeds can be sown without heat, germination taking the same time. When the seedlings are large enough to handle, transplant to a prepared site in the garden at a distance of 30cm (12in).

Division
The daughter plants are produced on runners and easily propagated by division, each having its own small root system. These can be taken off and replanted where required during the growing season from spring to early autumn.

Pests and Diseases
Obvious pests are slugs and birds, followed closely by children, and at flower shows by members of the public. With all of these there is not a lot one can do, apart from growing enough so that it does not matter. If grown in containers the plants can suffer from mildew. Remove the affected parts and make sure there is plenty of light and air.

Maintenance
Spring: Sow seed. Divide runners.
Summer: Feed with liquid fertilizer.
Autumn: Divide runners if they have become invasive.
Winter: No need for protection.

Wild Strawberry
Fragaria vesca

WARNING

Strawberries may produce an allergic response.

CULINARY

Eat the fruit fresh in fruit salads or on their own with cream, or use in cakes, pies and syrups and to flavour cordials. If you have enough you can also make jam.

The leaves have a musky flavour and scent. A tea can be made from them, but it is better to combine them with other herbs.

MEDICINAL

The fruit of the wild strawberry (unlike the cultivated varieties) are good for anaemia, bad nerves and stomach disorders. They are also an astringent, diuretic, tonic and laxative.

The leaves can be used to make a gargle and mouthwash for sore gums and mouth ulcers. Strawberry leaf tea is said to be a good tonic for convalescence and is enjoyed by children.

Wild strawberry jam

Garden Cultivation

Wild strawberries prefer a good fertile soil that does not dry out in summer, and either full sun or shade. They grow well in woods and hedgerows and make a marvellous ground cover, the dainty white flowers standing out amongst bright green shiny leaves which, when dry, have a fragrance of musk. The tiny delicious summertime fruits are a terrific bonus and have a good flavour.

Feed regularly with a liquid fertilizer (high in potash) as soon as the fruit begins, following the manufacturer's instructions. Often regarded as a weed by tidy gardeners, if you cannot stand the idea of rampant strawberry plants grow the Alpine variety.

Harvest

Pick leaves as required. If needed for drying, pick before the fruit sets and dry.

Pick fruits as they ripen to eat fresh. They can be frozen.

CONTAINER GROWING

Being small plants they are marvellous in containers, window boxes, even those pots with holes in the side, and also hanging baskets, where the runners look most attractive, trailing over the edge. Use the bark, peat mix of compost. Water and feed with liquid fertilizer regularly, especially when the fruit begins to set.

OTHER USES

The strawberry is used extensively in the cosmetic industry in skin cream manufacture. Mash the fruit and extract juice to add to facepacks to whiten skin and lighten freckles.

Apply cut strawberries to washed face to ease slight sunburn – makes a lovely picture, if you get bored you can always eat them.

Galium odoratum (Asperula odorata)

SWEET WOODRUFF

Also known as New Mowed Hay, Rice Flower, Ladies in the Hay, Kiss Me Quick, Master of the Wood, Woodward and Woodrowell. From the family Rubiaceae.

This is a native of Europe and has been introduced and cultivated in North America and Australia. It grows deep in the woods and in hedgerows.

Records date back to the 14th century, when woodruff was used as a strewing herb, as bed-stuffing and to perfume linen.

On May Day in Germany, it is added to Rhine wine to make a delicious drink called 'Maibowle'.

SPECIES

Galium odoratum (Asperula odorata)
Sweet Woodruff
Hardy perennial. Ht 15cm (6in), spread 30cm (12in) or more. White, star-shaped flowers from spring to early summer. The green leaves are neat and grow in a complete circle around the stem. The whole plant is aromatic.

CULTIVATION

Propagation
Seed
To ensure viability only use fresh seed. Sow in early autumn into prepared seed or plug trays, and cover with compost. Water in well. Seeds require a period of stratification (page 216). Once the seedlings are large enough, either pot or plant out as soon as the young plants have been hardened off. Plant 10cm (4in) apart.

Root Cuttings
The rootstock is very brittle and every little piece will grow. The best time is after flowering in the early summer. Lay small pieces of the root, 2-4cm (1-1.5in) long, evenly spaced, on the compost in a seed tray. Cover with a thin layer of compost, and water. Leave in a warm place, and the woodruff will begin to sprout again. When large enough to handle, split up and plant out.

Pests and Diseases
This plant rarely suffers from pests and diseases.

Maintenance
Spring: Take root cuttings before flowering.
Summer: Dig up before the flowers have set, to check spreading.
Autumn: The plant dies back completely in autumn. Sow seeds.
Winter: Fully hardy plant.

Garden Cultivation
Ideal for difficult places or underplanting in borders, it loves growing in the dry shade of trees right up to the trunk. Its rich green leaves make a dense and very decorative ground cover, its underground runners spreading rapidly in the right situation.

It prefers a rich alkaline soil with some moisture during the spring.

Harvest
The true aroma (which is like new mowed hay) comes to the fore when it is dried. Dry flowers and leaves together in early summer.

CONTAINER GROWING

Make sure the container is large enough, otherwise it will become root-bound very quickly. The compost should be the bark, peat mix. Only feed with liquid fertilizer when the plant is flowering. Position the container in semi-shade and do not over-water.

CULINARY

Add the flowers to salads. Main ingredients for a modern day May Wine would be a bottle of hock, a glass of sherry, sugar, and strawberries, with a few sprigs of woodruff thrown in 1 hour before serving.

MEDICINAL

A tea made from the leaves is said to relieve stomach pain, act as a diuretic, and be beneficial for those prone to gall stones.

Sweet woodruff tea

WARNING

Consumption of large quantities can produce symptoms of poisoning, including dizziness and vomiting.

Hesperis matronalis

SWEET ROCKET

Also known as Damask Violet and Dame's Violet. From the family Cruciferae.

This sweet-smelling herb is indigenous to Italy. It can now be found growing wild in much of the temperate world as a garden escapee. The old Greek name *Hesperis* was used by Theophrastus, the Greek botantist (370–285 BC). It is derived from 'hesperos', meaning evening, which is when the flowers are at their most fragrant.

SPECIES

Hesperis matronalis
Sweet Rocket
Hardy biennial; very occasionally it will be a perennial, sending out new shoots from the root stock. Ht 60-90cm (2-3ft), spread 25cm (10in). The 4-petalled flowers are all sweetly scented and come in many colours – pink, purple, mauve and white – in the summer of the second year. The leaves are green and lance shaped.
There is a double-flowered form of this plant – *Hesperis matronalis Double Form*. It can only be propagated by cuttings or division and needs a more sandy loam soil than sweet rocket.

CULTIVATION

Propagation
Seed
Sow the seed in the autumn in prepared seed or plug trays, covering the seeds with Perlite. Winter the young plants in a cold greenhouse for planting out in the spring at a distance of 45cm (18in) apart. Propagated this way it may flower the first season as well as the second.

Pests and Diseases
This herb is largely free from pests and diseases.

White Rocket
Hesperis matronalis

Maintenance
Spring: Sow seed outdoors.
Summer: In the second year dead head flowers to prolong flowering.
Autumn: Sow seed under protection.
Winter: No need to protect.

Garden Cultivation
It likes full sun or light shade and prefers a well-drained fertile soil. The seed can be sown direct into a prepared site in the garden in late spring thinning to 30cm (12in) apart, with a further thinning to 45cm (18in) later on if need be.

Harvest
Pick leaves when young for eating. Pick flowers as they open for using fresh or for drying.

CONTAINER GROWING

Sweet rocket is a tall plant. It looks attractive if 3 or 4 1-year-old plants are potted together, positioned to make the most of the scent on a summer evening. Use the bark, peat, grit mix of compost and water well in summer months. No need to feed.

Purple Rocket
Hesperis matronalis

CULINARY

Young leaves are eaten occasionally in salads. Use sparingly because they are very bitter. The flowers look attractive tossed in salads. They can also be used to decorate desserts.

OTHER USES

Add dried flowers to potpourris for pastel colours and sweet scent.

Lonicera

HONEYSUCKLE

Also known as Woodbine, Beerbind, Bindweed, Evening Pride, Fairy Trumpets, Honeybind, Irish Vine, Trumpet Flowers, Sweet Suckle, and Woodbind. From the family Caprifoliaceae.

'Come into the garden, Maud,
I am here at the gate alone;
And the woodbine spices are wafted abroad,
And the musk of the rose is blown.'
Lord Alfred Tennyson (1809-1892)

Honeysuckle grows all over northern Europe including Britain and can also be found growing wild in North Africa, Western Asia and North America.

Honeysuckle, *Lonicera spp*, receives its common name from the old habit of sucking the sweet honey-tasting nectar from the flowers. Generically it is said to have been named after the 16th-century German physician, Lonicer.

Honeysuckle was among the plants that averted the evil powers abroad on May Day and took care of milk, the butter and the cows in the Scottish Highlands and elsewhere. Traditionally it was thought that if honeysuckle was brought into the house, a wedding would follow, and that if the flowers were placed in a girl's bedroom, she would have dreams of love.

Honeysuckle's rich fragrance has inspired many poets, including Shakespeare, who called it woodbind after its notorious habit of climbing up trees and hedges and totally binding them up.

'Where oxlips and the nodding violet grows
quite over-canopied with luscious woodbine . . .'
A Midsummer Night's Dream

The plant appeared in John Gerard's 16th-century herbal; he wrote that 'the flowers steeped in oil and set in the sun are good to anoint the body that is benummed and grown very cold'.

SPECIES

There are many fragrant climbing varieties of this lovely plant. I have only mentioned those with a direct herbal input.

Lonicera x americana
American Honeysuckle
Deciduous perennial. Ht up to 7m (23ft). Strongly fragrant yellow flowers starting in a pink bud turning yellow and finishing with orangish pink throughout the summer. The berries are red, and the leaves are green and oval, the upper ones being united and saucer-like.

Lonicera caprifolium
Deciduous perennial. Ht up to 6m (20ft). The buds of the fragrant flowers are initially pink on opening; they then change to a pale white/pink/yellow as they age and finally turn deeper yellow. Green oval leaves and red berries, which were once fed to chickens. The Latin species name, **caprifolium**, means goats' leaf, reflecting the belief that honeysuckle leaves were a favourite food of goats. This variety and **Lonicera periclymenum** can be found growing wild in hedgerows.

Lonicera periclymenum
Deciduous perennial. This is the taller grower of the two common European honeysuckles, and reaches a height of 7m (23ft). It may live for 50 years. Fragrant yellow flowers appear mid-summer to mid-autumn, followed by red berries. Leaves are oval and dark green with a bluish underside.

Lonicera etrusca
Etruscan Honeysuckle
Semi-evergreen perennial. Ht up to 4m (12ft). Fragrant, pale, creamy yellow flowers which turn deeper yellow to red in autumn and are followed by red berries. Leaves oval, mid-green, with a bluish underside. This is the least hardy of those mentioned here, and should be grown in sun on a south facing wall, and protected in winter where temperatures fall below -3°C (23°F).

Lonicera Etrusca
Etruscan honeysuckle

Lonicera japonica
Japanese Honeysuckle

Semi-evergreen perennial. Ht up to 10m (33ft). Fragrant, pale, creamy white flowers turning yellow as the season progresses, followed by black berries. The leaves are oval and mid-green in colour. In the garden it is apt to build up an enormous tangle of shoots and best allowed to clamber over tree stumps or a low roof or walls. Attempts to train it tidily are a lost cause. Still used in Chinese medicine today.

CULTIVATION

Propagation
Seed

Sow seed in autumn thinly on the surface of a prepared seed or plug tray. Cover with glass and winter outside. Keep an eye on the compost moisture and only water if necessary. Germination may take a long time, it has been known to take 2 seasons, so be patient. A more reliable alternative method is by cuttings.

Cuttings

Take from non-flowering, semi-ripe shoots in summer and root in a bark, grit, peat mix of compost. Alternatively, take hardwood cuttings in late autumn, leave the cuttings in a cold frame or cold greenhouse for the winter.

Layering

In late spring or autumn honeysuckle is easy to layer. Do not disturb until the following season when it can be severed from its parent.

Pests and Diseases

Grown in too sunny or warm a place, it can become infested with greenfly, blackfly, caterpillars and red spider mites. Use a horticultural soap, and spray the pests according to the manufacturer's instructions.

Maintenance

Spring: Prune established plants.
Summer: Cut back flowering stems after flowering. Take semi-hardwood cuttings.
Autumn: Layer established plants. Lightly prune if necessary.
Winter: Protect certain species in cold winters.

Garden Cultivation

This extremely tolerant, traditional herb garden plant will flourish vigorously in the most unpromising sites. Honeysuckle leaves are among the first to appear, sometimes mid-winter, the flowers appearing in very early summer and deepening in colour after being pollinated by the insects that feed on their nectar. Good as cover for an unsightly wall or to provide a rich summer evening fragrance in an arbour.

Plant in autumn or spring in any fertile, well-drained soil, in sun or semi-shade. The best situation puts its feet in the shade and its head in the sunshine. A position against a north or west wall is ideal or on the shady side of a support such as a tree stump, pole and pergola. Prune in early spring, if need be. Prune out flowering wood or climbers after flowering.

MEDICINAL

An infusion of the heavy perfumed flowers can be taken as a substitute for tea. It is also useful for treating coughs, catarrh and asthma. As a lotion it is good for skin infections.

Recent research has proved that this plant has an outstanding curative action in cases of colitis.

Warning: The berries are poisonous. Large doses cause vomiting.

Harvest

Pick and dry the flowers for potpourris just as they open. This is the best time for scent although they are their palest in colour.

Pick the flowers for use in salads as required. Again the best flavour is before the nectar has been collected, which is when the flower is at its palest.

CULINARY

Add flowers to salads.

CONTAINER GROWING

This is not a plant which springs to mind as a good pot plant, certainly not indoors. But with patience, it makes a lovely mop head standard if carefully staked and trained; use an evergreen variety like **Lonicera japonica**. The compost should be a peat, bark mix. Water and feed regularly throughout the summer and in winter keep in a cold frame or greenhouse and only water occasionally.

OTHER USES

Flowers are strongly scented for potpourris, herb pillows and perfumery. An essential oil was once extracted from the plant to make a very sweet perfume but the yield was extremely low.

Honeysuckle flowers in a fresh summer salad

Nepeta

CATMINT

Also known as Catnep, Catnip, Catrup, Catswart and Field Balm.
From the family Labiatae.

Catmint *Nepeta racemosa*

Native to Europe and East and West Asia, but now naturalized in other temperate zones.

The species name may have derived from the Roman town Nepeti, where it was said to grow in profusion.

The Elizabethan herbalist, Gerard, recorded the source of its common name: 'They do call it *herba cataria* and *herba catti* because cats are very much delighted herewith for the smell of it is so pleasant unto them, that they rub themselves upon it and wallow or tumble in it and also feed on the branches and leaves very greedily.'

This herb has long been cultivated both for its medicinal and seasoning properties, and in the hippie era of the late '60s and '70s for its mildly hallucinogenic quality when smoked.

SPECIES

Nepeta cataria, **Nepeta x faassenii** and **Nepeta racemosa** are all called catmint, which can be confusing. However the first is the true herb with the medicinal and culinary properties and, just to be more confusing, is known also as dog mint!

Nepeta racemosa (mussinii)
Hardy perennial. Ht and spread 50cm (20in). Spikes of lavender blue/purple flowers from late spring to autumn. Small, mildly fragrant, greyish leaves. Marvellous edging plant for tumbling out over raised beds or softening hard edges of stone flags. Combines especially well with old-fashioned roses.

Nepeta camphorata
Hardy perennial. Ht and spread 60-75cm (24-30in). Very different from ordinary catmint and very fragrant. Tiny white blooms all summer. Small, silvery grey, aromatic foliage. Prefers a poor, well-drained, dryish soil, not too rich in nutrients, and full sun. However, it will adapt to most soils except wet and heavy.

Nepeta x faassenii
Hardy perennial. Ht and spread 45cm (18in). Loose spikes of lavender blue flowers from early summer to early autumn. Small greyish-green aromatic leaves form a bushy clump.

Nepeta cataria
Dog mint, Nep-in-a-hedge.
Hardy perennial. Ht 1m (3ft), spread 60cm (2ft). White to pale pink flowers from early summer to early autumn. Pungent aromatic leaves. This plant is the true herb. In the 17th century it was used in the treatment of barren women.

CULTIVATION

Propagation
Seed
Sow its small seed in spring or late summer, either where the plant is going to flower or onto the surface of pots, plug or seed trays. Cover with Perlite. Gentle bottom heat can be of assistance. Germination takes from 10-20 days, depending on the time of year (faster in late summer). Seed is viable for 5 years. When large enough to handle, thin the seedlings to 30cm (12in). The seed of **N. camphorata** should be sown in autumn to late winter. This seed will usually flower the following season.

Cuttings
Take softwood cuttings from new growth in late spring through to mid-summer. Do not choose flowering stems.

Catmint 'Six Hills Giant'
Nepeta 'Six Hills Giant'

Catmint *Nepeta cataria*

Division
A good method of propagation particularly if a plant is becoming invasive. But beware of cats! The smell of a bruised root is irresistible. Cats have been known to destroy a specimen replanted after division. If there are cats around, protect the newly divided plant.

Pests and Diseases
These plants are aromatic and not prone to pests. However, in cold wet winters, they tend to rot off.

Maintenance
Spring: Sow seeds.
Summer: Sow seeds until late in the season. Cut back hard after flowering to encourage a second flush.
Autumn: Cut back after flowering to maintain shape and produce new growth. If your winters tend to be wet and cold, pot up and winter this herb in a cold frame.
Winter: Sow seeds of **Nepeta camphorata**.

Garden Cultivation
The main problem with catmint is the love cats have for it. If you have ever seen a cat spaced-out after feeding (hence catnip) and rolling on it, then you will understand why cat lovers love catmint, and why cat haters who grow it get cross with cat neighbours. The reason why cats are enticed is the smell; it reminds them of the hormonal scent of cats of the opposite sex. With all this in mind, choose your planting site carefully.
   Nepeta make very attractive border or edging subjects. They like a well drained soil, sun, or light shade. The one thing they dislike is a wet winter, they may well rot off.
   Planting distance depends on species, but on average plant 50cm (20in) apart. When the main flowering is over, catmint should be cut back hard to encourage a second crop and to keep a neat and compact shape.

CULINARY

Use freshly picked young shoots in salads or rub on meat to release their mintish flavour. Catmint was drunk as a tea before China tea was introduced into the West. It makes an interesting cup!

MEDICINAL

Nepeta cataria is now very rarely used for medicinal purposes. In Europe it is sometimes used in a hot infusion to promote sweating. It is said to be excellent for colds and flu and children's infectious diseases, such as measles. It soothes the nervous system and helps get a restless child off to sleep. It also helps to calm upset stomachs and counters colic, flatulence and diarrhoea.
   In addition, an infusion can be applied externally to soothe scalp irritations, and the leaves and flowering tops can be mashed for a poultice to be applied to external bruises.

COMPANION PLANTING

Planting **Nepeta cataria** near vegetables deters flea beetle.

CONTAINER GROWING

N. x faassenii and **N. racemosa** look stunning in large terracotta pots. The grey green of the leaves and the blue-purple of the flowers complement the terracotta, and their sprawling habit in flower completes the picture. Use a well-draining compost, such as a peat, grit, bark mix. Note: both varieties tend to grow soft and leggy indoors.

OTHER USES

Dried leaves stuffed into toy mice will keep kittens and cats amused for hours.
   The scent of catnip is said to repel rats, so put bunches in hen and duck houses to discourage them.
   The flowers of **Nepeta x faassenii**, and **Nepeta racemosa** are suitable for formal displays.

Origanum

OREGANO &
MARJORAM

***Also known as Wild Marjoram, Mountain Mint, Winter Marjoram, Winter Sweet, Marjolaine and Origan.
From the family Labiatae.***

For the most part these are natives of the Mediterranean region. They have adapted to many countries, however, and a native form can now be found in many regions of the world, even if under different common names. For example, *Origanum vulgare* growing wild in Britain is called wild marjoram (the scent of the leaf is aromatic but not strong, the flowers are pale pink); while in Mediterranean countries wild *Origanum vulgare* is known as oregano (the leaf is green, slightly hairy and very aromatic, the flowers are similar to those found growing wild in Britain).

Pot Marjoram *Origanum onites*

Oregano is derived from the Greek 'oros' meaning mountain and 'ganos' meaning joy and beauty. It therefore translates literally as 'joy of the mountain'. In Greece it is woven into the crown worn by bridal couples.

According to Greek mythology, the King of Cyprus had a servant called Amarakos, who dropped a jar of perfume and fainted in terror. As his punishment the gods changed him into oregano, after which, if it was found growing on a burial tomb, all was believed well with the dead. Venus was the first to grow the herb in her garden.

Aristotle reported that tortoises, after swallowing a snake, would immediately eat oregano to prevent death, which gave rise to the belief that it was an antidote to poison.

The Greeks and Romans used it not only as scent after taking a bath and as a massage oil, but also as a disinfectant and preservative. More than likely they were responsible for the spread of this plant across Europe, where it became known as marjoram. The New Englanders took it to North America, where there arose a further confusion of nomenclature. Until the 1940s, common marjoram was called wild marjoram in America, but is now known as oregano. In certain parts of Mexico and the southern states of America, oregano is the colloquial name for a totally unrelated plant with a similar flavour.

Sweet marjoram, which originates from North Africa, was introduced into Europe in the 16th century and was incorporated in nosegays to ward off the plague and other pestilence.

Wild Marjoram
Origanum vulgare

SPECIES

Origanum amanum

Hardy perennial. Ht and spread 15-20cm (6-8in). Open, funnel-shaped, pale pink or white flowers borne above small heart-shaped, aromatic, pale green leaves. Makes a good alpine house plant. Dislikes a damp atmosphere.

Origanum x applei (heraceleoticum)
Winter Marjoram

Half-hardy perennial. Ht 23cm (9in), spread 30cm (12in). Small pink flowers. Very small aromatic leaves which, in the right conditions, are available all year round. Good to grow in a container.

Origanum dictamnus
Ditany of Crete

Hardy perennial. Ht 12-15cm (5-6in), spread 40cm (16in). Prostrate habit, purplish pink flowers that appear in hop-like clusters in summer. The leaves are white and woolly and grow on arching stems. Pretty little plant, quite unlike the other **origanums** in appearance. Tea made from the leaves is considered a panacea in Crete.

Golden Marjoram
Origanum vulgare 'Aureum'

Origanum 'Kent Beauty'

Hardy perennial. Ht 15-20cm (6-8in), spread 30cm (12in). Whorls of tubular pale pink flowers with darker bracts appear in summer on short spikes. Round, oval and aromatic leaves on trailing stems, which give the plant its prostrate habit and make it suitable for a wall or ledge. Decorative more than culinary.

Origanum laevigatum

Hardy perennial. Ht 23-30cm (9-12in), spread 20cm (8in). Summer profusion of tiny, tubular, cerise/pink/mauve flowers, surrounded by red/purple bracts. Aromatic, dark green leaves, which form a mat in winter. Decorative more than culinary.

Origanum laevigatum 'Herrenhausen'

Hardy perennial. Ht and spread 30cm (12in). Pink/mauve flowers which develop from deep purple buds in summer. Dark green, aromatic, slightly hairy leaves, with a pink tinge underneath. Decorative, and culinary when no other is available.

Greek Oregano
Origanum vulgare spp.

Origanum majorana (Origanum hortensis)
Sweet Marjoram

Also known as Knotted Marjoram or Knot Marjoram Half-hardy perennial. Grown as an annual in cool climates. Ht and spread 30cm (12in). Tiny white flowers in a knot. Round pale green leaves, highly aromatic. This is the best variety for flavour. Use in culinary recipes that state marjoram. The leaf is also good for drying, retaining a lot of its scent and flavour.

Origanum onites
Pot Marjoram

Hardy perennial. Ht and spread 45cm (18in). Pink/purple flowers in summer. Green aromatic leaves that form a mat in winter. Good grower with a nice flavour. Difficult to obtain the true seed; grows easily from cuttings, however.

Origanum rotundifolium

Hardy perennial. Ht 23-30cm (9-12in), spread 30cm (12in). Prostrate habit. The pale pink, pendant, funnel-shaped flowers appear in summer in whorls surrounded by yellow/green bracts. Leaves are small, round, mid-green, and aromatic. Decorative more than culinary.

Origanum vulgare
Oregano

Also known as Wild Marjoram

Hardy perennial. Ht and spread 45cm (18in). Clusters of tiny tubular mauve flowers in summer. Dark green, aromatic, slightly hairy leaves, which form a mat in winter. When grown in its native Mediterranean, it has a very pungent flavour, which bears little resemblance to that obtained in the cooler countries. When cultivated in the garden it becomes similar to pot marjoram.

Origanum vulgare spp.
Greek Oregano

Hardy perennial. Ht and spread 45cm (18in). Clusters of tiny tubular white flowers in summer. Grey/green hairy leaves, which are very aromatic and excellent to cook with.

Origanum vulgare 'Aureum'
Golden Marjoram

Hardy perennial. Ht and spread 45cm (18in). Clusters of tiny tubular mauve/pink flowers in summer. Golden, aromatic, slightly hairy leaves, which form a mat in winter. The leaves have a warm aromatic flavour when used in cooking; combines well with vegetables.

Compact Marjoram
Origanum vulgare 'Compactum'

Origanum vulgare 'Aureum Crispum'
Golden Curly Marjoram

Hardy perennial. Ht and spread 45cm (18in). Clusters of tiny tubular mauve/pink/white flowers in summer. Leaves, small, golden, crinkled, aromatic and slightly hairy, which form a mat in winter. The leaves have a slightly milder savoury flavour (sweeter and spicy) that combines well with vegetable dishes.

Origanum vulgare 'Compactum'
Compact Marjoram

Hardy perennial. Ht 15cm (6in), spread 30cm (12in). Lovely large pink flowers. Smallish green aromatic leaves, which form a mat in winter, have a deliciously warm flavour and combine well with lots of culinary dishes.

Origanum vulgare 'Gold Tip'
Gold Tipped Marjoram

Also known as Gold Splash Hardy perennial. Ht and spread 30cm (12in). Small pink flowers in summer. The aromatic leaves are green and yellow variegated. Choose the garden site carefully: shade prevents the variegation. The leaves have a mild savoury flavour.

Origanum vulgare 'Nanum'
Dwarf Marjoram

Hardy perennial. Ht 10cm (4in), spread 15cm (6in). White/pink flowers in summer. Tiny green aromatic leaves. It is a lovely, compact, neat little bush, great in containers and at the front of a herb garden. Good in culinary dishes.

CULTIVATION

Propagation
Seed
The following can be grown from seed: **Origanum vulgare**, **Origanum majorana**, **Origanum vulgare spp.** (Greek). The seed is very fine, so sow in spring into prepared seed or plug trays. Use the cardboard trick. Leave uncovered and give a bottom heat of 15°C (60°F). Germination can be erratic or 100 per cent successful. Watering is critical when the seedlings are young; keep the compost on the dry side. As the seed is so fine thin before pricking out to allow the plants to grow. When large enough, either pot on, using the bark, grit, peat mix of compost, or if the soil is warm enough and you have grown them in plugs, plant into the prepared garden.

Cuttings
Apart from the 3 species mentioned above, the remainder can only be propagated successfully by cuttings or division.
Softwood cuttings can be taken from the new growing tips of all the named varieties in spring. Use the bark, grit mix of compost.

Division
A number of varieties form a mat during the winter. These lend themselves to division. In spring, or after flowering, dig up a whole clump and pull sections gently away. Each will come away with its own root system. Replant as wanted.

Pests and Diseases
Apart from occasional frost damage, marjorams and oreganos, being aromatic, are mostly pest free.

Maintenance
Spring: Sow seeds. Divide established plants. Take softwood cuttings.
Summer: Trim after flowering to prevent plants becoming straggly. Divide established plants in late summer.
Autumn: Before they die down for winter, cut back the year's growth to within 6cm (2½in) of the soil.
Winter: Protect pot grown plants and tender varieties.

Garden Cultivation
Sweet marjoram and winter marjoram need a sunny garden site and a well-drained, dry, preferably chalk, soil. Otherwise plant them in containers. All the rest are hardy and adaptable, and will tolerate most soils as long as they are not waterlogged in winter. Plant gold varieties in some shade to prevent the leaves from scorching. For the majority, a good planting distance is 25cm (10in), closer if being used as an edging plant.

Harvest
Leaves
Pick leaves whenever available for use fresh. They can be dried or frozen, or be used to make oil or vinegar.

Flowers
The flowers can be dried just as they open for dried flower arrangements.

CONTAINER GROWING

The **Origanum** species look great in containers. Use the bark, grit, peat mix of compost. Make sure that they are not over-watered and that the gold and variegated forms get some shade at midday. Cut back after flowering and give them a liquid fertilizer feed.

Red mullet with tomatoes and oregano

CULINARY

Marjoram and oregano aid the digestion, and act as an antiseptic and as a preservative.
They are among the main ingredients of bouquet garni, and combine well with pizza, meat and tomato dishes, vegetables and milk-based desserts.

Red Mullet with Tomatoes and Oregano
Serves 4-6

4-6 red mullet, cleaned
3 tablespoons olive oil
1 medium onion, sliced
1 clove garlic, chopped
500g (1lb) tomatoes, peeled and chopped
1 green or red pepper, seeded and diced
1 teaspoon sugar
1 teaspoon chopped fresh oregano or ½ teaspoon dried oregano
Freshly milled salt and pepper
Oil for baking or shallow frying

Rinse the fish in cold water and drain on kitchen paper. Heat the olive oil in a pan and cook the onion and garlic slowly until golden brown; add the tomatoes, pepper, sugar and oregano, and a little salt and pepper.

Bring to the boil, then simmer for 20 minutes until thickened.
Bake or fry the fish. Brush them with oil, place in an oiled ovenproof dish and cook at a moderately hot temperature, 190°C (375°F, Gas Mark 5) for 7-8 minutes. Serve with the sauce.

MEDICINAL

This plant is one of the best antiseptics owing to its high Thymol content.
Marjoram tea helps ease bad colds, has a tranquil-lizing effect on nerves, and helps settle upset stomachs. It also helps to prevent sea sickness.
For temporary relief of toothache, chew the leaf or rub a drop of essential oil on the gums. A few drops of essential oil on the pillow will help you sleep.

OTHER USES

Make an infusion and add to the bath water to aid relaxation.

Centhranthus ruber (Valeriana ruber)

RED VALERIAN

Also known as American Lilac, Bloody Butcher, Bouncing Bess and Bouncing Betsy. From the family Valerianaceae.

A native of central and southern Europe cultivated widely in temperate climates, this cheerful plant was a great ornament in Gerard's garden, but he described it in 1597 as 'not common in England'. However, by the early 18th century it had become well known.

SPECIES

Centhranthus ruber (Valeriana ruber)
Red Valerian
Perennial. Ht 60-90cm (2-3ft), spread 45-60cm (18-24in). Showy red fragrant flowers in summer. They can also appear in all shades of white and pink. Fleshy, pale green, pointed leaves.

CULTIVATION

Propagation
Seed
Sow the small seeds in early autumn in seed or plug trays, using the bark, peat, grit mix of compost. Cover lightly with compost and leave outside over winter, covered with glass. As soon as you notice it germinating, remove the glass and place in a cold greenhouse. Prick the seedlings out when large enough to handle and pot up using the same mix of compost. Leave the pots outside for the summer, watering regularly until the autumn. No need to feed with liquid fertilizer. Plant out 60cm (2ft) apart.

Pests and Diseases
This plant does not suffer from pests or diseases.

Maintenance
Spring: Dig up self-sown seedlings and replant if you want them.
Summer: Dead head to prevent self-seeding.
Autumn: Sow seeds. Plant previous year's seedlings.
Winter: A very hardy plant.

Garden Cultivation
Red valerian has naturalized on banks, crumbly walls and rocks in coastal regions. It is very attractive to butterflies. As an ornamental, it thrives in poor, well-drained, low fertile soil, and especially on chalk or limestone. It likes a sunny position and self-seeds prolifically.

Harvest
Dig complete root up in the late autumn of the second and third years. Wash and remove the pale fibrous roots, leaving the edible rhizome. If you want to dry this rhizome, cut it into manageable slices (see drying). Pick young leaves as required.

CONTAINER GROWING

Make sure the container is large enough and use a soil-based compost. No need to feed, otherwise you will inhibit its flowers. Position the container in a sunny spot and water regularly.

CULINARY

Very young leaves are eaten in France and Italy. They are incredibly bitter.

Red Valerian
Centhranthus ruber

MEDICINAL

A drug is obtained (by herbalists only) from the root, which looks like a huge radish and has a characteristic odour. It is believed to be helpful in cases of hysteria and nervous disorders because of its sedative and anti-spasmodic properties.

WARNING

Large doses or extended use may produce symptoms of poisoning. Do not take for more than a couple of days at a time.

Pulmonaria officinalis

LUNGWORT

Also known as Jerusalem Cowslip, Abraham, Isaac and Jacob, Adam and Eve, Bedlam, Cowslip, Beggar's Basket, Bottle of Allsorts, Children of Israel, Good Friday Plant, Lady's Milk, Lady Mary's Tears, Spotted Mary, Thunder and Lightening, Virgin Mary, Virgin Mary's Milkdrops and Virgin Mary's Tears, Spotted Bugloss, Jerusalem Sage, Maple Lungwort, Spotted Comfrey and Spotted Lungwort. From the family Boraginaceae.

Lungwort is a native plant of Europe and northern parts of the USA. It has naturalized in many countries in cool climates, where it grows in shady, moist areas and in woodlands. The markings on the leaves were attributed to the Virgin Mary's milk or her tears; however, the generic name, *Pulmonaria*, comes from 'pulmo' meaning lung, and the common name, Lungwort, conjurs up a rather different image – of diseased lungs – to those blotched markings on the leaves. The Doctrine of Signatures, which held that all plants must be associated either by appearance, smell or habit with the disease which it was said to heal, used it for various lung disorders.

SPECIES

Pulmonaria augustifolia
Hardy perennial. Ht 23cm (9in), spread 20-30cm (8-12in). Flowers pink turning to bright blue in spring. Leaves lance shaped and mid-green with no markings.

Pulmonaria longifolia
Hardy perennial. Ht 30cm (12in), spread 45cm (18in). The flowers start pinkish turning purplish-blue in spring. The leaves are lance shaped, dark green, and slightly hairy with white spots.

Pulmonaria officinalis
Lungwort
Semi-evergreen hardy perennial. Ht 30cm (12in), spread 60cm (24in). Pink flowers turning blue in spring. Leaves oval with blotchy white/cream markings on a mid-green, slightly hairy surface.

Lungwort *Pulmonaria officinalis* **in flower**

Pulmonaria officinalis 'Sissinghurst White'
Semi-evergreen hardy perennial. Ht 30cm (12in), spread 45-60cm (18-24in). White flowers in spring. Leaves white-spotted, mid-green in colour, with a pointed oval shape.

Pulmonaria rubra 'Red Start'
Semi-evergreen hardy perennial. Ht 30cm (12in), spread 60cm (24in). Pink/red flowers in spring. The leaves are long ovals, velvety and mid-green with no markings.

Pulmonaria saccharata 'Mrs Moon'

Semi-evergreen hardy perennial. Ht 30cm (12in), spread 60cm (24in). Flowers start as pink and turn blue in spring. The green leaves are long pointed ovals with clear, creamy white, variable spots.

Note: The American native Virginian cowslip, **Mertensia virginica,** also known as smooth lungwort, belongs to the same Boraginaceae family as Lungwort. The flowers are purple/blue and the leaves lance shaped. It is excellent for shady places. The foliage dies back very early in autumn and leaves a bare patch, so it is not suitable for front of border. Propagate in the same way as the **Pulmonaria spp**.

CONTAINER GROWING

Make sure the container is large enough to give the creeping rhizomes a chance to spread and so prevent the plant from becoming pot bound too quickly. Use a soil-based compost and a frost-hardy container, as these plants do not like coming inside even into a cold greenhouse, where the growth becomes soft and rots off. During the growing season keep the container in a shady spot and water well.

MEDICINAL

Lungwort is a soothing expectorant. The silica it contains restores the elasticity of the lungs. Externally it has been used for healing all kinds of wounds.

Lungwort potpourri

CULTIVATION

Propagation
Seeds
Lungwort seldom produces viable seed; increase your stock by division, but watch out in the garden, where it will self-seed erratically.

Division
Divide established plants either after flowering in late spring or in the autumn.

Pests and Diseases
Lungwort can suffer from powdery mildew when the leaves die back in autumn. Simply remove the damaged leaves and dispose of them.

Maintenance
Spring: Dig up seedlings which mysteriously appear in odd parts of the garden.
Summer: Do nothing.
Autumn: Divide established plants. Cut back growth.
Winter: No need to protect, fully hardy.

Lungwort
Pulmonaria officinalis

Garden Cultivation
This attractive, fully hardy plant prefers a moist but well-drained soil with added leaf mould or well-rotted manure. It is an ideal plant for shady parts of the garden but will tolerate most situations. Plant out 30cm (12in) apart in the autumn. Lungwort grows quickly and spreads to provide dense ground cover. Water freely in dry weather.

Harvest
Pick the leaves after flowering in the summer and dry for medicinal use.

'How can a man grow old who has sage in his garden?'
Ancient Proverb

Salvia

SAGE

From the family Labiatae

This large family of over 750 species is widely distributed throughout the world. It consists of annuals, biennials and perennials, herbs, sub-shrubs and shrubs of various habits. It is an important horticultural group. I have concentrated on the medicinal, culinary and a special aromatic species.

The name Salvia is derived from the Latin 'salveo' meaning I save or heal, because some species have been highly regarded medicinally.

The Greeks used it to heal ulcers, consumption, and snake bites. The Romans considered it a sacred herb to be gathered with ceremony. A special knife was used, not made of iron because sage reacts with iron salts. The sage gatherer had to wear clean clothes, have clean feet and make a sacrifice of food before the ceremony could begin. Sage was held to be good for the brain, the senses and memory. It also made a good gargle and mouthwash and was used as a toothpaste.

There are many stories about why the Chinese valued it so highly, and in the 17th century Dutch merchants found that the Chinese would trade 3 chests of China tea for 1 of sage leaves.

Above: **Sage** *Salvia officinalis*

Right: **Purple Sage** *Salvia officinalis Purpurascens Group*

SPECIES

I have only chosen a very few species to illustrate, they are the main ones used in cooking and medicine – with one exception, with which I begin.

Salvia elegans 'Scarlet Pineapple' (rutilans)
Pineapple Sage
Half-hardy perennial. Ht 90cm (3ft), spread 60cm (2ft). Striking red flowers, mid- to late summer. The leaves are green with a slight red tinge to the edges and have a glorious pineapple scent. This sage is sub-tropical and must be protected from frost during the winter. In temperate climates it is basically a house plant and if kept on a sunny windowsill can be used throughout the year. It can only be grown from cuttings. This is an odd sage to cook with, it does not taste as well as it smells. It is fairly good combined with apricots as a stuffing for pork, otherwise my culinary experiments with it have not met with great success.

Salvia lavandulifolia
Narrowed-Leaved Sage
Also known as Spanish Sage. Hardy evergreen perennial. Ht and spread 45cm (18in). Attractive blue flowers in summer. The leaves are green with a texture, small, thin, and oval in shape and highly aromatic. This is an excellent sage to cook with, very pungent. It also makes a good tea. Can only be grown from cuttings.

Salvia officinalis
Sage
Also known as Common Sage, Garden Sage, Broad Leaved Sage, and Sawge. Hardy evergreen perennial. Ht and spread 60cm (2ft). Mauve/blue flowers in summer. The leaves are green with a texture, thin and oval in shape and highly aromatic. This is the best known sage for culinary use. Can be easily grown from seed. There is also a white flowering sage **Salvia officinalis 'Albiflora'**, which is quite rare.

Salvia officinalis Broad-leaved (latifolia)
Broad-Leaved Sage
Hardy evergreen perennial. Ht and spread 60cm (2ft). Very rarely flowers in cool climates, if it does they are blue/mauve in colour. The leaves are green with a texture, larger than the ordinary sage, with an oval shape and highly aromatic. Good for cooking. Can only be grown from cuttings.

Salvia officinalis icterina
Gold Sage
Hardy evergreen perennial. Ht 45cm (18in), spread 75cm (30in). Very rarely flowers in cool climates, if it does they are blue/mauve in colour. The leaves are green/gold variegated with a texture, small and oval in shape and aromatic. A mild flavour but equally good to cook with. Can only be grown from cuttings.

Clary Sage *Salvia sclarea*

Salvia sclarea
Clary Sage
Also known as Muscatel Sage.
Hardy biennial. Ht 60-90cm (2-3ft), spread 45cm (18in). Colourful flower bracts – blue/purple/lilac with a whitish base in summer. Leaves are often 20-23cm (8-9in) long, soft green in colour and slightly wrinkled. Easily grown from seed. There is another variety, **Salvia var. turkestanica**, with white flowers tinged with pink.

Salvia officinalis Purpurascens Group
Purple/Red Sage
Hardy evergreen perennial. Ht and spread 70cm (28in). Mauve/blue flowers in summer. The leaves are purple with a texture, a thin oval shape and aromatic. 2 points to think about.
If you clip it in the spring, it develops new leaves and looks really good but flowers only a small amount. If you do not clip it and allow it to flower it goes woody. If you then cut it back it does not produce new growth until the spring, so can look a bit bare. So what to do? There is also a variegated form of this purple sage **Salvia officinalis 'Purpurascens Variegata'**. Both of these can only be grown from cuttings.

Salvia officinalis 'Tricolor'
Tricolor Sage
Half-hardy evergreen perennial. Ht and spread 40cm (16in). Attractive blue flowers in summer. The leaves are green with pink, white and purple variegation, with a texture. They are small, thin, and oval in shape and highly aromatic. It has a mild flavour, so can be used in cooking. Can only be grown from cuttings.

CULTIVATION

Propagation
Seed
Common and clary sage grow successfully in the spring from seed sown into prepared seed or plug trays and covered with Perlite. The seeds are a good size. If starting off under protection in early spring, warmth is of benefit – temperatures of 15-21°C (60-70°F). Germination takes 2-3 weeks. Pot up or plant out when the frosts are over at a distance of 45-60cm (18-24in) apart.

Cuttings
This is a good method for all variegated species and the ones that do not set seed in cooler climates. Use the bark, peat mix of compost. *Softwood*: Take these cuttings in late spring or early summer from the strong new growth. All forms take easily from cuttings; rooting is about 4 weeks in summer. *Layering*: If you have a well-established sage, or if it is becoming a bit woody, layer established branches in spring or autumn.

Pests and Diseases
Sage grown in the garden does not suffer over much from pests and disease. Sage grown in containers, especially pineapple sage, is prone to red spider mite. As soon as you see this pest, treat with a liquid horticultural soap as per the instructions.

Maintenance
Spring: Sow seeds. Trim if needed, and then take softwood cuttings.
Summer: Trim back after flowering.
Autumn: Protect all half-hardy sages, and first-year plants.
Winter: Protect plants if they are needed for fresh leaves.

Purple Sage *Salvia officinalis Purpurascens Group* and **Gold Sage** *Salvia officinalis icterina*

Garden Cultivation
Sage, although predominately a Mediterranean plant, is sufficiently hardy to withstand any ordinary winter without protection, as long as the soil is well drained and not acid, and the site is as warm and dry as possible. The flavour of the leaf can vary as to how rich, damp, etc, the soil is. If wishing to sow seed outside, wait until there is no threat of frost and sow direct into prepared ground, spacing the seeds 23cm (9in) apart. After germination thin to 45cm (18in) apart. For the first winter cover the young plants with agricultural fleece or a mulch.
  To keep the plants bushy prune in the spring to encourage young shoots for strong flavour, and also after flowering in late summer. Mature plants can be pruned hard in the spring after some cuttings have been taken as insurance. Never prune in the autumn as this can kill the plant. As sage is prone to becoming woody, replace the plant every 4-5 years.

Sage Bianco *Salvia blancoana* **has a silvery leaf and prostrate habit**

Harvest

Since sage is an evergreen plant, the leaves can be used fresh any time of the year. In Mediterranean-type climates, including the southern states of America, the leaves can be harvested during the winter months. In cooler climates this is also possible if you cover a chosen bush with agricultural fleece as this will keep the leaves in better condition. They dry well, but care should be taken to keep their green colour. Because this herb is frequently seen in its dried condition people presume it is easy to dry. But beware, although other herbs may lose some of their aroma or qualities if badly dried or handled, sage seems to pick up a musty scent and a flavour really horrible to taste – better to grow it in your garden to use fresh.

CONTAINER GROWING

All sages grow happily in containers. Pineapple sage is an obvious one as it is tender, but a better reason is that if it is at hand one will rub the leaves and smell that marvellous pineapple scent. Use the bark, grit, peat mix of compost for all varieties, feed the plants after flowering, and do not over-water.

COMPANION PLANTING

Sage planted with cabbages is said to repel cabbage white butterflies. Planted next to vines it is generally beneficial.

OTHER USES

The dried leaves, especially those of pineapple sage, are good added to potpourris.

Broad-Leaved Sage *Salvia officinalis broad-leaved*

MEDICINAL

For centuries, sage has been esteemed for its healing powers. It is a first rate remedy as a hot infusion for colds. Sage tea combined with a little cider vinegar makes a gargle which is excellent for sore throats, *laryngitis and tonsillitis. It is also beneficial for infected gums and mouth ulcers.*

The essential oil, known as Sage Clary or Muscatel Oil, is obtained by steamed distillation of the fresh or *partially dried flower stems and leaves. It is used in herbal medicine but more widely in toilet waters, perfumes and soap, and to flavour wine, vermouth and liqueurs.*

Left: **Tricolor Sage** *Salvia officinalis 'Tricolor'*

CULINARY

This powerful healing plant is also a strong culinary herb, although it has been misused and misjudged in the culinary world. Used with discretion it adds a lovely flavour, aids digestion of fatty food, and being an antiseptic it kills off any bugs in the meat as it cooks. It has long been used with sausages because of its preservative qualities. It also makes a delicious herb jelly, or oil or vinegar. But I like using small amounts fresh. The original form of the following recipe comes from a vegetarian friend of mine. I fell in love with it and have subsequently adapted it to include some other herbs.

Hazelnut and Mushroom Roast
Serves 4

A little sage oil
Long grain brown rice (measured to the 150ml (5fl oz) mark on a glass measuring jug)
275ml (10fl oz) boiling water
1 teaspoon salt
1 large onion, peeled and chopped
110g (4oz) mushrooms, wiped and chopped
2 medium carrots, pared and roughly grated
½ teaspoon coriander seed
1 tablespoon soy sauce
110g (4oz) wholemeal breadcrumbs
175g (6oz) ground hazelnuts
1 teaspoon chopped sage leaves
1 teaspoon chopped lovage leaves
Sunflower seeds for decoration
A 900g (2lb) loaf tin, lined with greaseproof paper

Pre-heat the oven (180°C 350°F, Gas Mark 4).

Heat 1 dessertspoon of sage oil in a small saucepan, toss the rice in it to give it a coating of oil, add boiling water straight from the kettle and the teaspoon of salt. Stir, and let the rice cook slowly for roughly 40 minutes or until the liquid has been absorbed.

While the rice is cooking, heat 1 tablespoon of sage oil in a medium sized frying-pan, add the onions, mushrooms, carrots, the ground coriander seed and soy sauce. Mix them together and let them cook for about 10 minutes.

Combine the cooked brown rice, breadcrumbs, hazelnuts, sage and lovage; mix with the vegetables and place the complete mixture in the prepared loaf tin. Scatter the sunflower seeds on top and bake in the oven

Hazelnut and mushroom roast, a delicious dish for vegetarians

for 45 minutes. Leave to cool slightly in the tin. Slice and serve with a home-made tomato sauce and a green salad.

WARNING

Extended or excessive use of sage can cause symptoms of poisoning. Although the herb seems safe and common, it you drink the tea for more than a week or two at a time, its strong antiseptic properties can cause potentially toxic effects.

Santolina

COTTON LAVENDER

Also known as Santolina and French Lavender. From the family Compositae

Cotton lavender is a native of Southern France and the Northern Mediterranean area, where it grows wild on calcareous ground. It is widely cultivated, adapting to the full spectrum of European and Australian climates and to warm-to-hot regions of North America, surviving even an Eastern Canadian winter on well-drained soil.

The Greeks knew cotton lavender as 'abrotonon' and the Romans as 'habrotanum', both names referring to the tree-like shape of the flying branches. It was used medicinally for many centuries by the Arabs. And it was valued in medieval England as an insect and moth repellent and vermifuge.

The plant was probably brought into Britain in the 16th century by French Huguenot gardeners, who were skilled in creating the popular knot garden so popular among the Elizabethans. Cotton lavender was used largely in low clipped hedges, and as edging for the geometrical beds.

Cotton lavender Rosmarinifolia
Santolina rosmarinifolia rosmarinifolia

SPECIES

Despite its common name, this is not a member of the Lavandula family; rather it is a member of the daisy family.

Santolina chamaecyparissus
Cotton Lavender
Hardy evergreen perennial. Ht 75cm (2.5ft), spread 1m (3ft). Yellow button flowers from mid-summer to early autumn, silver coral like aromatic foliage.

Cotton Lavender
Santolina chamaecyparissus

Santolina chamaecyparissus 'Lemon Queen'
Cotton Lavender 'Lemon Queen'
As 'Edward Bowles', but feathery, deep cut grey foliage.

Santolina pinnata neapolitana 'Edward Bowles'
Cotton Lavender 'Edward Bowles'
Hardy evergreen perennial. Ht 75cm (2.5ft), spread 1m (3ft). Cream button flowers in summer. Feathery, deep cut, grey/green foliage.

Cotton Lavender 'Lemon Queen'
Santolina chamaecyparissus 'Lemon Queen'

Santolina pinnata ssp 'Neapolitana'
Cotton Lavender 'Neopolitana'
As 'Edward Bowles'.

Santolina rosmarinifolia rosmarinifolia 'Primrose Gem'
Cotton Lavender Primrose Gem
Hardy evergreen perennial. Ht 60cm (2ft), spread 1m (3ft). Pale yellow button flowers in summer. Finely cut green leaves.

Cotton Lavender Rosmarinifolia (Virens) (Holy Flax)
As 'Primrose Gem'. Bright yellow button flowers in summer. Finely cut, bright green leaves.

Cotton Lavender
Rosmarinifolia (Virens)

CULTIVATION

Propagation
Seed
Although seed is now available, it is erratic and not worth the effort as germination is poor.

Cuttings
Take 5-8cm (2-3in) soft stem cuttings in spring before flowering, or take semi-ripe stem cuttings from mid-summer to autumn. They root easily without the use of any rooting compound.

Pests and Diseases
Compost or soil that is too rich will attract aphids.

Maintenance
Spring: Cut straggly old plants hard back. Take cuttings from new growth.
Summer: I can not stress enough that after flowering the plants should be cut back or the bushes will open up and lose their attractive shape.
Autumn: Take semi-ripe cuttings, protect them from frost in a cold frame or greenhouse.
Winter: Protect in only the severest of winters.

Garden Cultivation
This elegant aromatic evergreen is ideal for the herb garden as a hedging or specimen plant in its own right. Plant in full sun, preferably in sandy soil. If the soil is too rich the growth will become soft and lose colour. This is particularly noticeable with the silver varieties.
Planting distance for an individual plant 45-60cm (18-24 in), for a hedging 30-38cm (12-15in). Hedges need regular clipping to shape in spring and summer. Do not cut back in the autumn in frosty climates, as this can easily kill the plants. If

temperatures drop below -15° C (5°F) protect with agricultural fleece or a layer of straw, spruce or bracken.

Harvest
Pick leaves and dry any time before flowering. Pick small bunches of flower stems for drying, in late summer. They can be dried easily by hanging the bunches upside down in a dry, airy place.

CONTAINER GROWING

Santolina can not be grown indoors, however as a patio plant, a single plant clipped to shape in a large terracotta pot can look very striking. Use a bark, peat compost. Place pot in full sun. Do not over-feed with liquid fertilizer or growth will be too soft.

CULINARY

Cotton lavender (**S. chamaecyparissus**) makes an interesting addition to shortbread biscuits instead of Rosemary. Interesting being the operative word.

MEDICINAL

Although not used much nowadays, it can be applied to surface wounds, hastening the healing process by encouraging scar formation. Finely ground leaves ease the pain of insect stings and bites.

OTHER USES
Lay in drawers, under carpets, and in closets to deter moths and other insects, or make a herbal moth bag.

Herbal Moth Bag

A handful of wormwood
A handful of spearmint
A handful of cotton lavender
A handful of rosemary
1 tablespoon of crushed coriander

Dry and crumble the ingredients, mix together and put in a muslin or cotton bag.

Tanacetum balsamita

ALECOST
(COSTMARY)

Other names: Bible Leaf, Sweet Mary and Mint Geranium. From the family Compositae

Alecost originated in Western Asia and by the time it reached America in the 17th century, Culpeper wrote of its use in Europe that 'Alecost is so frequently known to be an inhabitant of almost every garden, that it is needless to write a description thereof.'

Since then, in America it has escaped its garden bounds and grows wild in eastern and mid-west States, while in Europe it has become altogether rare. Only recently has interest revived among propagators as well as horticulturalists who, in the space of twenty years, have reclassified alecost twice, from *Chrysanthemum* to *Balsamita* and now to *Tanacetum*.

The first syllable of its common name, alecost, derives from the use to which its scented leaves and flowering tops were put in the Middle Ages, namely to clarify, preserve and impart an astringent, minty flavour to beer. The second syllable, 'cost', comes from *kostos*, Greek for 'spicy'. Literally, 'alecost' means 'a spicy herb for ale'.

The alternative, costmary, by introducing a proper name symbolic of motherhood, conveys another of the plant's traditional uses in the form of a tea.

Religious connotations extend to one other nickname, 'Bible Leaf', which grew out of the Puritan habit of using a leaf of the herb as a fragrant Bible bookmark, its scent dispelling faintness from hunger during long sermons.

SPECIES

**Tanacetum balsamita
(Balsamita major)**
Alecost (costmary)
Hardy perennial. Ht 1m
(3ft), spread 45cm (18in).
Small white yellow-eyed daisy
flowers mid- to late summer.
Large rosettes of oval
aromatic silvery green leaves.

**Tanacetum balsamita
tomentosum**
Camphor plant
Hardy perennial. Ht 1m
(3ft), spread 45cm (18in).
Appearance and habit very
similar to alecost, but unlike
the latter it is not palatable
as a culinary herb. Its leaves
are an effective moth
repellent.

Camphor plant *Tanacetum balsamita tomentosum*

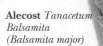

Alecost *Tanacetum Balsamita (Balsamita major)*

CULTIVATION

Propagation
Seed
The seed is fine and thin and cannot be propagated from plants grown in cool climates (the seed not being viable). Obtain seed from a specialist seedsman. Sow in spring onto the surface of a seed or plug tray and cover with Perlite. Use low warmth to encourage germination, and be patient! The seedlings may emerge in 10 days or 2 months, depending on the freshness of the seed. Pot on or plant out into the garden when they are large enough to handle.

Division
The best way to propagate is by division either in spring or autumn. Take a portion of the creeping root from an established plant, and either plant out or pot up using a bark, peat, grit mix of compost. If taking offsets in autumn, it is better to winter the pots in a cold frame.

Garden cultivation
Plant 60cm (2ft) apart and, if possible, in a sunny position. Both alecost and camphor plant will adapt to most conditions but prefer a rich, fairly dry and well-drained soil. Both species will grow in shade but may fail to bloom. But that is no great loss as the flower is not striking. Both die back in winter.

Pests and diseases
Leaves of both are aromatic, so pests are not a problem.

Maintenance
Spring: Divide established plants. Sow seed if available. Feed established plants.
Summer: Plant out seedlings early into permanent positions. Dead head.
Autumn: Trim back flowers. Remove offsets from established plants to prevent them encroaching into others' territory.
Winter: Tidy up dead leaves; they spread disease if left to rot. Bring in potted-up offsets.

Harvest
Pick the leaves for fresh culinary use any time. Both alecost and camphor leaves dry well and retain their sweet aroma. Pick for drying just before flowering for the strongest scent.

The flowers are not worth harvesting for drying.

Only in a warm climate is it worth collecting seeds. Do it when flowers turn brown and centre eye disintegrates on touch. Sow the following year (see Propagation).

CONTAINER GROWING

Neither species lends itself to container growing. They grow soft, prone to disease, are untidy when in flower, tend to be blown over by the wind and make untidy specimens in flower. If there is no other course, dead head to prevent from flowering and do not over-feed with liquid fertilizer.

Alecost *Tanacetum balsamita (Balsamita major)*

CULINARY

Use only the alecost leaf and very sparingly as it has a sharp tang which can be overpowering. Add finely chopped leaves to carrot soups, salads, game, poultry, stuffing and fruit cakes, or with melted butter to peas and new potatoes. Its traditional value to beer holds good for home brewing.

MEDICINAL

Traditionally in the form of a tea (Costmary or Sweet Mary Tea) to ease the pain of childbirth. It was also used as a tonic for colds, catarrh, stomach upsets and cramps. Rub a fresh leaf of alecost on a bee sting or horse fly bite to relieve pain.

Alecost with new potatoes

OTHER USES

Both alecost and camphor leaves, which are sweet scented like balsam, serve to intensify other herb scents and act as an insect repellent. Add to potpourris or to linen bags or with lavender to make nosegay sachets, or infuse to make a final scented rinse for hair.

Fresh or dried leaves of alecost can be added to baths for a fragrant and refreshing soak.

Alecost potpourri

Viola tricolor

HEARTSEASE

Also known as Wild Pansy, Field Pansy, Love Lies Bleeding, Love in Idleness, Herb Trinity, Jack Behind the Garden Gate, Kiss Me Behind the Garden Gate, Kiss Me Love, Kiss Me Love at the Garden Gate, Kiss Me Quick, Monkey's Face, Three Faces Under a Hood, Two Faces in a Hood and Trinity Violet. From the family Violaceae.

Heartsease is a wild flower in Europe and North America, growing on wasteland and in fields and hedgerows.

In the Middle Ages, due to the influence of Christianity and because of its tricolour flowers – white, yellow and purple – Heartsease was called Trinitaria or Trinitatis Herba, the herb of the Blessed Trinity.

In the traditional language of flowers, the purple form meant memories, the white loving thoughts, and the yellow, souvenirs.

SPECIES

Viola arvensis
Field Pansy
Hardy perennial. Ht 5-10cm (2-4in). The flowers are predominantly white or creamy, and appear in early summer. The green leaves are oval with shallow, blunt teeth.

Viola tricolor *Heartsease*

Viola lutea
Mountain Pansy
Hardy perennial. Ht 8-20cm (3-8in). Single coloured flowers in summer vary from yellow to blue and violet. The leaves are green and oval near the base of the stem, narrower further up.

Viola tricolor
Heartsease
Hardy perennial, often grown as an annual. Ht 15-30cm (6-12in). Flowers from spring to autumn. Green and deeply lobed leaves.

CULTIVATION

Propagation
Seed
Sow seeds under protection in the autumn, either into prepared seed, plug trays or pots. Do not cover rhe seeds. No bottom heat required. Winter the seedlings in a cold frame or cold greenhouse. In the spring harden off and plant out at a distance of 15cm (6in).

Maintenance
Spring: Sow seed.
Summer: Dead head flowers to maintain flowering throughout the season.
Autumn: Sow seed for early spring flowers.
Winter: No need to protect.

Garden Cultivation
Heartsease will grow in any soil, in partial shade or sun. Sow the seeds from spring to early autumn where they are to flower. Press into the soil but do not cover.

Harvest
Pick the flowers fully open – from spring right through until late autumn. Use fresh or for drying.

The plant has the most fascinating seed capsules, each capsule splitting into 3. The best time to collect seeds is midday when the maximum number of capsules will have opened.

CONTAINER GROWING

Heartsease look very jolly in any kind of container. Pick off the dead flowers as they appear to keep the plant flowering for longer.

CULINARY

Add flowers to salads and to decorate sweet dishes.

MEDICINAL

An infusion of the flowers has long been prescribed for a broken heart. Less romantically, it is also a cure for bed-wetting.

An ointment made from it is good for eczema and acne and also for curing milk rust and cradle cap.

Herbalists use it to treat gout, rheumatoid arthritis and respiratory disorders. An infusion of heartsease leaves added to bath water has proved beneficial to suffers of rheumatic disease.

Warning: In large doses, it may cause vomiting.

OTHER USES
Cleansing the skin and shampooing thinning hair.